'The Collection

Cures for the Common Cuisine

Blessed Offering
by John Cook

sponsored by

Tom Thumb

The Women's Auxiliary to Children's Medical Center of Dallas is a non-profit organization whose purpose is to render efficient and effective service to all units of the hospital and its patients. The Auxiliary selects special projects and programs for the benefit of the hospital and raises funds through means approved by the Children's Medical Center Board of Directors.

Copies of *The Collection* are available by filling out the order form found in the back of this book or by sending $25 plus $5 shipping and handling to:

Women's Auxiliary to Children's Medical Center of Dallas Cookbook
2777 Stemmons Freeway, Suite 1025
Dallas, Texas 75207
(214) 456-8371 Cookbook Voice Mail

You also can order online at: **www.childrens.com/cookbook**

A special thank you to Robert Best and Best Reprographics for providing John Cook's works of art to the Women's Auxiliary. Without his contribution this cookbook would not be complete.

At the time of production, the art in this cookbook was either owned by Robert Best or had not yet been purchased.

WIMMER
COOKBOOKS
ConsolidatedGraphics
1-800-548-2537

Contents

Brunch & Breads
9

Appetizers
21

Soups & Salads
41

Meat & Poultry
65

Game
97

Seafood
111

Vegetables & Condiments
125

Pasta, Rice & Potatoes
145

The Best Desserts
161

Children's Recipes
181

sponsored by

The Collection **3**

DEAR FRIENDS OF CHILDREN'S,

For more than 88 years, the Women's Auxiliary has been a generous and steadfast supporter of Children's Medical Center of Dallas. Through volunteerism and fund-raising, the organization plays a unique role in supporting the hospital's mission to make life better for children.

The Women's Auxiliary's impact on the lives of patients and their families is far reaching. The organization's dedication is visible in the hospital's critical care and surgical areas, where funds raised by the annual Family Night at Six Flags have purchased life-saving equipment. And, through volunteerism and other ventures, the group helps to comfort and serve families while they stay in our hospital. This is seen in the fall decorating project that brings more than 50 holiday trees to Children's and by operating the Children's Corner Gift Shop, where visitors may buy toys or get-well items for a child.

The efforts of the Women's Auxiliary and support from friends in the community will be crucial as the hospital moves forward and expands. Critical shortages in space, coupled with predictions for a 26 percent growth rate in the North Texas pediatric population in the next decade, necessitate action to handle current and future patient volumes.

Children's is now embarking upon an ambitious fund-raising initiative that will allow us to expand facilities, staff, research and education capabilities. The hospital's plans include adding floors to the main campus, constructing a new outpatient surgery center and building a second major facility in Plano to serve north Texas patients. Children's also is committed to expanding its already premier medical staff by attracting leading pediatricians and pediatric specialists to our facilities.

Though broad in scope, this growth is necessary to becoming one of the best children's hospitals in the nation. Children's is on track financially and developmentally, but there still is a good distance to go. The hospital will continue to rely on friends like the Women's Auxiliary and you to help ensure that North Texas children have access to the best possible care.

We are excited about the release of *The Collection* and what the funds generated by the sale of these cookbooks will do for Children's as the hospital expands to meet growing population demands. This project is reflective of the Women's Auxiliary's commitment to our hospital, and we thank you for your support of our mission to *make life better for the children.*

Sincerely,

George D. Farr
President and Chief Executive Officer
Children's Medical Center of Dallas

sponsored by

2001-2002 CHILDREN'S MEDICAL CENTER OF DALLAS BOARD OF TRUSTEES

A history of caring

Children's Medical Center of Dallas traces its roots to the summer of 1913 when a group of public health nurses began an open-air clinic for infants at a local park. Through much work and dedication on the part of medical volunteers in the community, the clinic eventually grew into the Bradford Memorial Hospital for Babies, which merged with Children's Hospital of Texas and the Richmond Freeman Memorial Clinic in 1948 to form Children's.

And, in 1962, the auxiliaries of each of the formerly separate hospitals formed one group, the Women's Auxiliary to Children's, to support the new hospital.

The spirit of those Dallas healthcare pioneers is evident at Children's today, where everything from the atmosphere to complex pediatric research projects is aimed at fulfilling the hospital's mission — to make life better for children. And when parents bring their children to the hospital for treatment, they avail them of the benefits of the Children's mission.

Children's, which is nationally ranked today and is on track to becoming one of the nation's best pediatric healthcare systems, is the only healthcare facility in Dallas dedicated exclusively to treating children from birth to age 18 for a variety of diseases and disorders. Patients receive care ranging from a simple eye exam to specialized treatments in numerous areas, including heart disease, hematology-oncology and cystic fibrosis. In addition, Children's is a major pediatric transplant center for kidney, liver, heart and bone marrow. The hospital also operates a system of more than 50 outpatient specialty clinics that provide a comprehensive range of specialized medical care.

Children's is one of only 14 national pediatric research centers sanctioned by the National Institutes of Health. Through an affiliation with The University of Texas Southwestern Medical Center, the Children's medical staff conducts research that is instrumental in developing treatments, therapies and greater understanding of pediatric diseases.

As a not-for-profit healthcare institution, Children's ensures its patients that every decision is aimed at improving patient care, not at benefiting stockholders.

Children's enjoys a stellar reputation as one of the finest pediatric facilities in the United States, recognized by organizations such as the Joint Commission on Accreditation of Healthcare Organizations and by *Child* magazine. But the hospital's service to the thousands of children who come each year to be treated for various ailments continues to be the its primary concern, therefore making life better for children.

sponsored by

NeimanMarcus

A prayer for children

We pray for the children
who put chocolate fingers on everything,
who love to be tickled,
who stomp in puddles and ruin new pants,
who eat candy before supper,
who can never find their shoes in the morning.

And we also pray for those
who stare at photographers from behind barbed wire,
who have never bound down the street in a new pair of shoes,
who never played "one potato, two potatoes,"
who are born in places that we would not be caught dead in and they will be.

We pray for the children
who give us sticky kisses and fistfuls of dandelions,
who sleep with their dog and who bury their goldfish,
who hug us so tightly and who forget their lunch money,
who squeeze toothpaste all over the sink,
who watch their fathers shave,
who slurp their soup.

And we pray for those
who will never get dessert,
who have no favorite blanket to drag around behind them,
who watch their fathers suffer,
who cannot find any bread to steal,
who do not have any rooms to clean up,
whose pictures are on milk cartons instead of on dressers,
whose monsters are real.

We pray for the children
who spend all their allowance by Tuesday,
who pick at their food,
who love ghost stories,
who shove their dirty clothes under the bed and never rinse the bathtub,
who love visits from the Tooth Fairy, even after they find out who it really is,
who do not like to be kissed in front of the school bus,
who squirm during services.

And we also pray for those children
whose nightmares occur in the daytime,
who will eat anything,
who have never seen a dentist,
who are not spoiled by anyone,
who go to bed hungry and wake up hungry,
who live and move and have no address.

We pray for those children
who like to be carried and for those children who will have to be carried,
for those who give up and for those who never give up,
for those that will grab the hand of anyone kind enough to offer it,
for those who find no hand to grab.

For all these children, we pray today, for they are so precious.

Reprinted with permission by Ina J. Hughs

About the artist

Texas artist John Cook paints with a passion, compelled to capture Impressionist images on canvas or watercolor paper. "I see beauty in God's creation, and I strive to capture a glimpse of that perfection in paint," Cook says.

Cook began his fine art career in 1990 at the age of 49, inspired early by the paintings of Russian-American artist Nicolai Fechin. Later influences include artist John Singer Sargent, Frank Brangwyn and Winslow Homer, as well as the still life and florals of Henry Fatin Latour.

By drawing with a brush rather than a pencil, Cook achieves the loose and free style that characterizes his work. Never belabored, each painting reflects his passion to catch a mood with interplay of light and shade. Nothing is too large or small to attempt, as reflected in his diverse range of subject matter: from still life to portraits to landscapes, architecture and native Texas-Western imagery. "A kind of impatient realism," is how Cook describes his paintings. Action and energy permeate his canvases and there is a spontaneous nature to his work that retells the artist's need to quickly achieve the essence of light as it dances, pierces, careens, and bounces to find its way throughout the subject. Cook states, "as for my style, if I could do a painting in less than sixty seconds I would be pleased. Sometimes I feel the urgency to attack a canvas and capture the intensity of my mind and emotions without respecting the necessary effort for the image to be valued as 'fine art.'" Trips to London, Paris, San Francisco and Belgium produced many of Cook's paintings.

Born in 1941 in Dallas, Cook grew up near Highland Park and attended school at the University of Arlington and the Art Center School of Los Angeles. In his initial career as an illustrator, Cook's work was in demand by advertising agencies and their high-profile clients including American Airlines, CBS, Neiman Marcus and Disney Epcot Center. In 1990, he put aside his illustrator's pens and inks and pursued his heart's desire: a career as a painter. Married to a school teacher for 31 years and a deeply religious, devoted family man, Cook says, "painting is not the most important thing in my life, but it is a close second."

COOKBOOK EXECUTIVE STEERING COMMITTEE

Honorary Co-Chairmen
Jane Dunne
Randi Halsell

1998-2001 Co-Chairmen
Brenda Cockerell
DeeDee Lee

2001-2002 Co-Chairmen
Jill Dardick
Devin Rambie

2002-2003 Co-Chairmen
Michele McDermett
Devin Rambie

**1998-2001
Recipe Testing Chairman**
Tanya Mendenhall

Treasurer
Jane Switzer

Sponsor Chairman
Ann Delatour

**Children's Medical
Center Advisors**
Linda Harris
Jill Hassmann

Recipe Copy Editors
Brenda Cockerell
DeeDee Lee

Advisory Chairmen
Leslie Golden
Betsy MacKay
Elizabeth Naftalis, M.D.
Allison Woram
Kimberly Yamanouchi, M.D.

COOKBOOK STEERING COMMITTEE

Special Events Chairman
Kay Weeks

Retail Sales Chairman
Tamareh Tuma

2002 Auxiliary President
Cordelia Boone

Special Events Assistant Chairman
Leslie Ficke

Distribution Co-Chairmen
Pam Brock
Martha Hooper

2001 Auxiliary President
Devin Rambie

Public & Media Relations
Brynn Bagot

Physician Sponsor Chairman
Sue Hubbard, M.D.

2000 Auxiliary President
Susan Farris

Design Coordinator
Karee Sampson

Communications Chairman
Anne Collins

1999 Auxiliary President
Sandra Cude

Group Sales Chairmen
Amara Durham
Karen Sargent

Print Production Coordinator
Laura Humphries

**1998 Auxiliary President
Founding Cookbook President**
Debbie Snell

sponsored by

Granite

Golden Moments
by John Cook

sponsored by

Notes...

- *When using natural cheeses, finely shred to increase melting times. A well-chilled cheese will shred more easily than a cheese that has been sitting at room temperature.*
- *Remove bread loaves from the pans as soon as baked. If allowed to cool in the pans, the bread may continue to cook and the bottom may become soggy. Cool on wire racks for best results.*
- *A foil lining placed under the cloth in a breadbasket helps to keep breads warm.*

Brunch & Breads

Blueberry Coffee Cake   10

Breakfast Crumb Cake   10

Baked French Toast   11

Quiche Lorraine.   11

Quiche with Almonds.   12

Ham and Grits Quiche   13

Delicious Egg Casserole   13

Eggs Magda.   14

Santa Fe Soufflé.   14

Sugared Bacon.   14

Sausage Cheese Biscuits   15

Angel Biscuits   15

Cinnamon Muffins   16

Banana Nut Bread   16

Old-Fashioned Gingerbread   17

S&S Tearoom Strawberry Bread   17

Light and Tasty Cornbread   18

Chocolate Chip Zucchini Bread   18

Potato Rolls.   19

Spicy Pecan Cheese Wafers   19

Blueberry Coffee Cake

Batter:

1	cup butter, softened	2	cups all-purpose flour
2	cups sugar	1	teaspoon baking powder
2	eggs, beaten	1/4	teaspoon salt
1	cup sour cream	1	cup frozen blueberries, thawed and drained
1	tablespoon vanilla		

Filling:

1/2 cup brown sugar
1 tablespoon cinnamon
1/2 cup chopped nuts

Preheat oven to 350 degrees. Cream butter and sugar until fluffy. Add eggs and next 5 ingredients, mixing well. Fold in blueberries and set aside. Mix brown sugar, cinnamon and nuts in small bowl. Pour half of batter into oiled Bundt pan. Sprinkle filling over the batter. Repeat layers. Gently swirl mixture with a knife for marbling. Bake at 350 degrees for 1 hour. Yields 10-12 servings.

Breakfast Crumb Cake

2	cups all-purpose flour	1	cup buttermilk
2	cups brown sugar	1	teaspoon baking soda
1/3	cup butter	1	teaspoon vanilla
1/3	cup shortening		Chopped pecans, optional
1	egg		

Preheat oven to 350 degrees. Combine flour, sugar, butter and shortening in large bowl. Set aside 3/4 cup for topping. Add egg, buttermilk, baking soda and vanilla to bowl. Mix well. Grease and flour a 13x9x2-inch baking pan. Pour batter into pan; sprinkle with reserved topping and pecans, if desired. Bake for 30 minutes. Yields 10-12 servings.

note...

Best if prepared one day before serving.

Sausage Cheese Biscuits

1   package (16 ounce) hot sausage, at room temperature
1   pound sharp cheese, shredded
½   teaspoon salt
3   cups biscuit baking mix

Combine all ingredients in large bowl. Form into small balls and lightly flatten. Place on baking sheet and bake at 375 degrees for 12 to 14 minutes. Yields 10-12 servings.

Angel Biscuits

4   cups biscuit baking mix
1   carton (8 ounce) sour cream
¾   cup club soda
½   cup butter, softened and divided

Preheat oven to 450 degrees. Combine baking mix, sour cream, club soda and ¼ cup butter in mixing bowl. Turn out dough onto floured cutting board. Knead 1 minute. Roll out dough to ½ to ¾-inch thickness. Cut out biscuits. Melt remaining butter in a 9x13-inch glass casserole dish. Arrange biscuits in dish and bake for 12 to 14 minutes. If desired, tops of warm biscuits may be brushed with additional butter before serving. Yields 8-10 servings.

note...
● This recipe
freezes well.

Cinnamon Muffins

5	tablespoons butter, softened	1/4	teaspoon salt
1	cup sugar, divided	1/4	teaspoon nutmeg
1	egg	1/2	cup milk
1 1/2	cups all-purpose flour	6	tablespoons butter, melted
2 1/4	teaspoons baking powder	1	tablespoon cinnamon

Preheat oven to 350 degrees. Cream softened butter, 1/2 cup sugar and egg in large bowl with an electric mixer. Sift together flour, baking powder, salt and nutmeg. Add to creamed mixture alternately with milk. Fill prepared miniature muffin pans halfway with batter. Bake for 20 minutes. Combine remaining 1/2 cup sugar with cinnamon and set aside. Remove muffins from pans. Dip tops of muffins into melted butter. Roll muffin tops in cinnamon mixture. Yields 1 dozen.

Banana Nut Bread

● This is a rich, dense bread that is best served the next day. It also freezes well.

1 1/2 cups sugar
1/2 cup shortening
2 eggs
1/2 teaspoon salt
1 teaspoon baking soda dissolved in 2 tablespoons hot water
2 cups all-purpose flour
4-6 bananas (extremely ripe)
1 cup pecans

Preheat oven to 250 degrees. In food processor cream sugar and shortening. Add eggs and salt, processing until mixed well. Add baking soda and water mixture. Add and process flour, bananas and pecans until nuts are chopped. Pour into greased and floured loaf pan and bake for 1 1/2 hours or until done in center. Yields 1 large loaf.

Old-Fashioned Gingerbread

½ cup shortening
½ cup butter
1 cup sugar
2½ cups sifted all-purpose flour
1 rounded teaspoon cloves
1 rounded teaspoon cinnamon
1 rounded teaspoon allspice
½ teaspoon ginger
1 rounded teaspoon baking soda
½ teaspoon salt
1 cup molasses
2 egg yolks
2 egg whites, beaten
1 cup boiling water

Preheat oven to 350 degrees. Cream shortening, butter and sugar in large bowl with an electric mixer. Add flour and next 6 ingredients, beating well. Add molasses and continue to beat. Add egg yolks, then beaten egg whites. Add boiling water, continuing to beat. Pour into greased and floured 10x7-inch baking pan. Bake for 35 minutes. Yields 8-10 servings.

S&S Tearoom Strawberry Bread

3 cups sifted all-purpose flour
1 teaspoon baking soda
1 teaspoon salt
1 tablespoon cinnamon
2 cups sugar
4 eggs, beaten
1½ cups cooking oil
2 cups strawberries, coarsely chopped
1¼ cups chopped pecans

Sift together flour and next 4 ingredients and set aside. Mix oil and eggs; add to flour mixture, stirring just enough to moisten. Fold in strawberries and pecans. Pour into 2 greased and floured loaf pans. Bake at 350 degrees for 1 hour. Cool 5 minutes before removing from pans. Finish cooling on wire racks. Yields 2 loaves.

Light and Tasty Cornbread

3	cups cornmeal	1	teaspoon baking soda
1	cup all-purpose flour	1	teaspoon baking powder
¾	cup sugar	½	cup shortening, melted
1	teaspoon salt	3	cups buttermilk

Preheat oven to 350 degrees. Combine all ingredients and mix well. Spoon into oiled 10-inch tube pan; let mixture rest 10 minutes. Bake for 1 hour or until done. Cool 5 minutes before removing from pan. Yields 12 servings.

Chocolate Chip Zucchini Bread

3	eggs	3	teaspoons cinnamon
1	cup cooking oil	3	teaspoons vanilla
2	cups sugar	1	cup chocolate chips
2	cups all-purpose flour	1	cup chopped pecans
1	teaspoon salt	1	cup chopped walnuts
1	teaspoon baking soda	2	cups grated zucchini, unpeeled
¾	teaspoon baking powder		

Preheat oven to 350 degrees. Blend eggs and next 8 ingredients together in large bowl. Fold in chocolate chips, nuts and zucchini, mixing well. Pour into 2 greased and floured loaf pans. Bake for 50 minutes to 1 hour. Yields 2 loaves.

Potato Rolls

1/2 cup sugar
4 cups cooked potatoes, mashed
2 cups milk, scalded
1 cup butter
4 eggs

2 yeast cakes
8-9 cups all-purpose flour, divided
4 teaspoons salt, divided
1/4 cup butter, melted

note...
Bake frozen rolls
within one month.

Add sugar to mashed potatoes. After scalding milk, add butter; combine potato mixture and milk mixture. Add eggs one at a time, mixing well after each addition. Cool to room temperature, then crumble yeast cakes on top. Let stand 35 minutes or until bubbly. Measure flour in 2-cup increments, adding 1 teaspoon salt to each 2 cups flour. Incorporate flour mixture into potato mixture until dough consistency; add more flour if necessary. Place dough in greased bowl and let rise until doubled. Punch down and roll out to 1/2-inch thickness; cut with biscuit cutter. Dip one-half of biscuit in melted butter and fold over. Place on baking sheet lined with waxed paper and place in freezer. Once frozen, transfer to plastic freezer bags. Bake in glass casserole dish at 400 degrees for 10 minutes or until golden brown. Yields 3 baking sheets of rolls.

Spicy Pecan Cheese Wafers

1 pound extra sharp
    cheese, grated
1 cup butter, softened
1 cup finely chopped pecans

1/2 teaspoon cayenne pepper
1 teaspoon salt
2 1/2 cups all-purpose flour
2-3 tablespoons hot sauce

Blend cheese and butter thoroughly. Add pecans, cayenne, salt and flour and mix well. Shape into four (8-inch) logs. Wrap tightly in waxed paper and chill until ready to bake. Slice 1/8-inch thick and place on oiled baking sheet. Bake at 350 degrees for 15 to 20 minutes. Yields 2-3 dozen.

The Professional
by John Cook

sponsored by

GALLERIA

Notes...

- *Fresh herbs provide a pizzazz unmatched by dried herbs. When purchasing fresh herbs, select those with a clean, fresh fragrance and bright color.*
- *To curl fresh vegetables such as celery and carrots, cut the vegetables lengthwise into strips and soak in ice water until serving time.*

Appetizers

Blue Cheese Biscuit Bites	22	
Easy Cheese Wafers	22	
Warm Blue Cheese Appetizers	22	
Sugar and Nut Glazed Brie	23	
Hot Pineapple Scallop	23	
Curried Cheese Wedges	23	
Spinach-Artichoke Cheesecake	24	
Last Minute Spinach Balls	25	
Basil Parmesan Spread	25	
Party Salmon Mousse	26	
Jumbo Lump Crabmeat Dip	26	
Crabmeat Cream Puffs	27	
Shrimp Ceviche	27	
Hot Crab and Artichoke Dip	28	
Shrimp Cocktail Acapulco Style	28	
Shrimp and Gruyère Tart	29	
Fantastic Caviar Torte	30	

Curried Shrimp Dip 31
Party Shrimp Mold 31
Easy and Delicious Crab Mold 32
Provençal Goat Cheese Gratin 33
Summertime Tomato Blue Cheese Spread . . . 34
Pesto and Sun-Dried Tomato Torte 34
Avocado Terrine 35
Sun-Dried Tomatoes and Feta Terrine 35
Fiesta Cheesecake 36
Confetti Bagel Bites 36
Jalapeño Cheese Dip 37
Beef Queso Dip 37
Southwestern Poolside Dip 38
Tasty Corn and Green Chili Dip 38
Salsa Verde 39
Avocado Corn Guacamole 39
Artichoke Chili Dip 40

Blue Cheese Biscuit Bites

1   can (8 ounce) biscuits, quartered
1/4-1/2 cup butter, melted
3/4   cup crumbled blue cheese

Preheat oven to 350 degrees. Brush bottom of glass baking dish with some melted butter.
Arrange biscuits evenly apart in dish. Drizzle with remaining butter and sprinkle with cheese.
Bake for 10 to 15 minutes or until browned and bubbly. Yields 32 bites.

note...

• *Parmesan or Cheddar cheese may be substituted for blue cheese.*

Easy Cheese Wafers

2   cups all-purpose flour
1   cup butter, softened
2   cups shredded Cheddar cheese
2   cups crispy rice cereal

In large bowl combine all ingredients well. Shape into logs, wrap in plastic wrap and chill. Cut into
1/4-inch slices and transfer to a lightly oiled baking sheet. Bake at 350 degrees for 15 to 20 minutes.
Yields 2-3 dozen.

• *Cheese wafers freeze well.*

Warm Blue Cheese Appetizers

1   package (8 ounce) cream cheese, softened
1   package (4 ounce) blue cheese, crumbled
1/2   cup half-and-half
2   garlic cloves, finely crushed
7   bacon slices, cooked and crumbled

Combine cheeses, mixing well. Transfer to food processor; add half-and-half and garlic; pulse.
Fold in bacon and transfer mixture into lightly oiled baking dish. Bake at 350 degrees for 15 minutes.
Serve in warm chafing dish with melba rounds, crackers or chips. Yields 30-40 servings.

Sugar and Nut Glazed Brie

¼ cup packed brown sugar
¼ cup sliced almonds
1 tablespoon whiskey or cognac

1 (14 ounce) Brie wheel
1 box wheat wafers
2 apples, cut into wedges, optional

Combine sugar, almonds and whiskey or cognac. Cover and chill until ready to prepare. Place cheese in large round ovenproof dish or 9-inch pie plate. Top cheese with sugar mixture. Bake at 500 degrees for 5 minutes or until lightly browned. Serve with apple wedges or wheat wafers. Yields 25-30 servings.

Hot Pineapple Scallop

2 cans (20 ounce) crushed pineapple
6 tablespoons pineapple juice, reserved
2 cups shredded Cheddar cheese
6 tablespoons all-purpose flour

1 cup sugar
1 box round buttery crackers
½ cup butter, melted

Drain pineapple, reserving 6 tablespoons juice. In large bowl combine reserved juice, pineapple, cheese, flour and sugar, mixing well. Pour into a lightly oiled casserole or chafing dish. Crush 1 sleeve of crackers. Place on top of pineapple. Pour butter over crackers. Bake at 350 degrees for 45 minutes. Serve with remaining buttery crackers. Yields 30-40 servings.

Curried Cheese Wedges

2 cups shredded sharp Cheddar cheese
1½ cups green onions, chopped
2 cups black olives, chopped
1 teaspoon garlic salt

1 teaspoon pepper
1 cup mayonnaise
½ teaspoon curry powder
6 English muffins, split

Combine cheese and next 6 ingredients, mixing well. Spread on each half of muffin. Cut each muffin half into quarters. Arrange quarters on baking sheet and freeze. Transfer from baking sheet to plastic freezer bags. Bake wedges as needed at 375 degrees for 15 to 20 minutes. Yields 72 pieces.

Spinach-Artichoke Cheesecake

Crust:

2   cups finely crushed tortilla chips
¼   cup butter, melted

Preheat oven to 325 degrees. Combine chips and butter; press onto bottom and sides of lightly buttered 9-inch springform pan. Bake for 10 minutes. Set aside to cool.

Filling:

1   onion, finely chopped
2   garlic cloves, minced
2   tablespoons butter
2   packages (10 ounce) frozen chopped spinach, thawed and squeezed dry
2   cans (14 ounce) artichoke hearts, drained and coarsely chopped
1   jar (4 ounce) diced pimiento, drained

3   packages (8 ounce) cream cheese, softened
1   package (8 ounce) feta cheese, drained
⅓   cup milk
4   large eggs
1   teaspoon salt
½   teaspoon cayenne pepper
1   teaspoon black pepper
1   carton (16 ounce) sour cream

In skillet sauté onion and garlic in butter until tender. Combine with spinach, artichokes and pimiento and set aside. Beat cream cheese at medium speed with electric mixer until creamy. Drain feta and finely crumble. Add to cream cheese, beating until well blended. Add milk; add eggs one at a time, beating after each addition. Stir in salt, cayenne and black pepper; add spinach mixture, mixing well. Pour into crust. Bake at 325 degrees for 1 hour, 10 minutes or until set. Cool 10 minutes. Gently spread sour cream over top. Bake for additional 15 minutes. Cool, then chill until ready to serve. Serve with tortilla chips and hot sauce or pico de gallo. Yields 40-50 servings.

Last Minute Spinach Balls

2	packages (10 ounce) frozen chopped spinach		2	cups cornbread stuffing mix
1	onion, finely chopped		4	eggs, beaten
2-3	garlic cloves, minced		1/2	cup Parmesan cheese, grated
3/4	cup butter, melted		1/4	teaspoon thyme
				Pepper to taste

Cook and drain spinach well; set aside. In small skillet sauté onion and garlic in butter. Add spinach, stuffing mix and remaining ingredients, mixing well. Shape into bite-size balls, place on baking sheet and freeze overnight. Bake frozen at 350 degrees for 20 minutes or until lightly browned. Yields 48 servings.

Basil Parmesan Spread

1   cup loosely packed, coarsely chopped spinach leaves
1   cup loosely packed fresh basil leaves, chopped
1   teaspoon minced garlic
1/4 cup olive oil
1   cup Parmesan cheese, grated
Salt and pepper to taste
1   package (8 ounce) cream cheese, softened
4   ounces goat cheese, at room temperature
1/4 cup finely chopped walnuts, divided
1/4 cup sliced or chopped oil packed sun-dried tomatoes, drained and divided
1   box crackers or bagel chips

Place spinach, basil and garlic in food processor and pulse. Add oil and Parmesan cheese and process until smooth. Add salt and pepper to taste and set aside. In mixing bowl combine cream cheese and goat cheese until well mixed. Line a 3-cup bowl (3-4 inches deep) with plastic wrap. Spread 1/3 of cream cheese mixture into prepared bowl. Spread half of spinach mixture over cheese layer. Layer half of walnuts over spinach. Top with half of sun-dried tomatoes. Repeat layers. Top with remaining 1/3 of cream cheese mixture. Fold over plastic wrap and press gently to pack down; chill overnight. Invert onto serving plate and remove plastic wrap. Allow spread to rest 30 minutes before serving. Serve with favorite crackers or bagel chips. Yields 10 servings.

note...
Spinach Balls may be prepared in advance and kept in freezer bags up to 3 months.

note...

- *Mousse is best when prepared one day before serving.*

Party Salmon Mousse

1 package (¼ ounce) unflavored gelatin	¼ teaspoon paprika
¼ cup cold water	1 teaspoon salt
½ cup boiling water	3 tablespoons finely chopped dill
½ cup mayonnaise	1 can (14¾ ounce) red salmon, skin and bones removed, or fresh poached salmon
Juice of ½ lemon	
½ small onion, finely grated	1 cup heavy cream, whipped
8 dashes of hot sauce	

Soften gelatin in cold water in large mixing bowl. Stir in boiling water and whisk until gelatin dissolves. Mix in mayonnaise and next 6 ingredients. Stir to blend thoroughly. Finely flake salmon; add to gelatin mixture. In separate bowl whip heavy cream to stiff peaks. Fold gently into salmon mixture. Transfer mixture to a 6 to 8-cup bowl or decorative mold. Cover and chill at least 4 hours or overnight. Serve with fresh toast points or table wafers. Yields 12 servings.

Jumbo Lump Crabmeat Dip

- *Fold crabmeat in very gently so that the lumps will not be broken.*

1 small yellow onion, minced	½ cup freshly grated Parmesan cheese
½ cup butter, divided	1 teaspoon garlic salt
1 package (8 ounce) cream cheese	Dash of white pepper
1 pound jumbo lump crabmeat	Dash of cayenne pepper
1½ cups heavy cream	Hot sauce to taste

In medium saucepan sauté minced onion in 1 tablespoon butter until transparent. Add remaining butter and cream cheese; simmer over low heat until melted. Add crabmeat and mix thoroughly. Gradually add heavy cream to mix. Stir in Parmesan, then add garlic salt, white pepper, cayenne pepper and hot sauce. Serve hot with toast points. Yields 12-14 servings.

Crabmeat Cream Puffs

Puffs:

½ cup butter
1 cup boiling water
1 cup all-purpose flour

¼ teaspoon salt
4 eggs

Preheat oven to 450 degrees. Melt butter in boiling water. Add flour and salt, stirring vigorously until mixture is smooth and forms a soft ball that does not separate. Cool mixture slightly. Add eggs one at a time, beating vigorously after each addition. Drop mixture by teaspoonfuls onto lightly oiled baking sheet. Bake for 5 minutes, then cool.

Crabmeat Mixture:

1½ cups fresh lump crabmeat
2 cups shredded
   sharp Cheddar cheese
2 cups mayonnaise

2 tablespoons Worcestershire sauce
2 teaspoons hot sauce
½ tablespoon minced onion
½ cup chopped celery

Combine crabmeat and remaining ingredients thoroughly and chill. Make a small slit in each cream puff. Fill with crabmeat mixture. Heat until cheese begins to melt. Yields 3 dozen.

note...

- *Packaged puff pastry may be substituted for the recipe. Cut into small squares or rounds and bake according to package directions.*

- *Top the puff pastry with a small amount of cheese and crabmeat mixture. Heat until cheese begins to melt.*

Shrimp Ceviche

1½ pounds cooked shrimp,
   peeled and coarsely chopped
Juice of 10 limes
1 tomato, diced
1 onion, diced
3-4 celery stalks, diced
1 green bell pepper,
   seeded and diced

3-4 jalapeño peppers,
   seeded and finely chopped
4 bay leaves
1 teaspoon oregano
1½ teaspoons salt
1 teaspoon pepper
¼ cup chopped cilantro

Place shrimp in non-metallic bowl. Cover with lime juice and marinate overnight. Drain shrimp, reserving juice. Combine shrimp and remaining ingredients. Add back ⅓ of reserved juice to shrimp mixture. Chill several hours and serve. Shrimp will keep up to 5 days in refrigerator. Yields 6-8 servings.

note...

The dip may be prepared one day in advance before baking.

Hot Crab and Artichoke Dip

1	large green bell pepper, seeded and chopped
1	tablespoon cooking oil
2	cans (14 ounce) artichoke hearts, drained and chopped
2	cups mayonnaise
½	cup green onions, sliced
½	cup chopped pimiento, drained

1	cup Parmesan cheese, grated
2	tablespoons lemon juice
3	tablespoons Worcestershire sauce
3	tablespoons pickled jalapeños, chopped
1	teaspoon celery salt
1	pound lump crabmeat
	Cayenne pepper to taste
	Pita triangles or Melba toast

Preheat oven to 375 degrees. In small skillet sauté bell pepper in oil over moderate heat, stirring until tender. In large bowl combine the bell pepper and next 9 ingredients. Gently fold in crabmeat. Transfer mixture to ovenproof chafing dish or baking dish. Bake for 25 to 30 minutes or until golden and bubbly. Serve with pita triangles or Melba toast. Yields 14 servings.

Shrimp Cocktail Acapulco Style

2	cups ketchup
2	cups spicy vegetable juice
2	tomatoes, chopped
1	onion, chopped
1	bunch chopped cilantro
	Juice of 3 limes
1	jalapeño pepper, diced

3	tablespoons chopped parsley
	Juice of 1 lemon
	Salt to taste
	Freshly ground black pepper to taste
2	pounds cooked shrimp, peeled
3	avocados, diced
	Saltine crackers

Mix all ingredients except avacados and chill. Add avocado to shrimp mixture just before serving. Serve chilled with saltine crackers. Yields 40-50 servings.

Shrimp and Gruyère Tart

Tart:

1¼ cups round buttery
    cracker crumbs

¼ cup butter, melted

1½ pounds medium fresh shrimp,
    peeled, deveined and chopped

½ green bell pepper, seeded
    and finely chopped

½ red bell pepper, seeded
    and finely chopped

1 small onion, finely chopped

2 garlic cloves, minced

3 tablespoons butter, melted

2 packages (8 ounce)
    cream cheese, softened

½ cup mayonnaise

4 eggs

⅓ cup milk

1¼ cups grated Gruyère cheese,
    packed slightly

1 teaspoon white pepper

Combine cracker crumbs and ¼ cup melted butter; press into bottom of 9-inch springform pan and set aside. In skillet sauté shrimp and next 4 ingredients in 3 tablespoons butter 4 to 5 minutes. Drain well and set aside. Beat cream cheese and mayonnaise with electric mixer at high speed until light and fluffy; add eggs, one at a time, beating after each addition. Gradually add milk, beating at low speed just until blended. Stir in shrimp mixture, Gruyère and white pepper. Pour mixture into prepared springform pan. Bake at 300 degrees for 1 hour, 20 minutes, to 1 hour, 30 minutes, or until set. Turn oven off and partially open oven door; leave in oven 1 hour. Let cool on wire rack. Serve at room temperature. Garnish with whole or chopped shrimp and red pepper strips if desired. Serve with Italian Tomato Sauce. Yields 40-50 servings.

Italian Tomato Sauce:

1 medium onion, chopped

2 garlic cloves, minced

1 tablespoon olive oil

3 cans (14 ounce) tomatoes,
    drained and chopped

1 can (15 ounce) tomato sauce

3 teaspoons Italian seasoning

3 bay leaves

Sauté onion and garlic in hot oil in large skillet until tender. Add tomatoes and remaining ingredients. Simmer, uncovered, 20 minutes or until most of liquid evaporates, stirring occasionally. Remove bay leaves and serve warm.

Fantastic Caviar Torte

8   hard cooked eggs, peeled and sliced
1/4   cup mayonnaise
1/4   cup parsley, chopped
1/4   teaspoon salt
1/4   teaspoon pepper
2   tablespoons coarse grain Dijon mustard
1   cup chopped green onions, divided
2   cups cooked and chopped shrimp

4   packages (3 ounce) cream cheese, softened and divided
1/2   cup bacon bits
1/4   cup white wine
1/2   cup sour cream
2   ounces drained red caviar
2   ounces drained black caviar
2   ounces drained golden caviar
Chopped parsley, for garnish
1   box Melba toast

Butter the bottom and sides of a 9-inch springform pan. Process eggs and next 5 ingredients in food processor. Spread mixture evenly into prepared 9-inch springform pan. Sprinkle 1/2 of green onions over egg mixture and set aside. Process shrimp, 1 package cream cheese, bacon bits and wine in a clean processor bowl. Spread over green onions. Sprinkle remaining green onions over shrimp mixture. In a clean processor bowl process remaining 3 packages cream cheese until smooth and blend in sour cream. Pour over green onions. Cover tightly with plastic wrap and chill at least 3 hours or preferably overnight. With a sharp knife, loosen torte from pan. Remove side of pan and place torte on serving dish. Spread drained caviars in desired pattern on top. Press chopped parsley around top edge of torte. Serve with toast points or Melba toast. Yields 40-50 servings.

Curried Shrimp Dip

2 packages (8 ounce)
low fat cream cheese, softened
1 sweet onion, minced
1 red bell pepper,
seeded and minced
2 cups frozen cooked salad shrimp,
thawed, rinsed and drained
Juice of $1/2$ lemon

$1/2$ cup dry roasted salted peanuts, chopped
$1^1/2$ teaspoons curry powder
3 hard cooked eggs, finely chopped
$1/2$ teaspoon salt
Freshly ground black pepper to taste
1-2 jars mango chutney
2 boxes water crackers or Melba toast

Combine cream cheese, onion and bell pepper in bowl, mixing well. Refresh rinsed and drained shrimp with lemon juice. Add shrimp and remaining ingredients to cheese mixture, mixing well. Line bowl or mold with plastic wrap and coat with nonstick cooking spray. Pour into bowl and press down gently to fill. Chill 4 hours or preferably overnight. To serve, invert bowl on serving platter and remove plastic wrap. Pour mango chutney over shrimp mold. Serve additional chutney on the side along with water crackers or Melba toast. Yields 30-40 servings.

Party Shrimp Mold

1 package ($1/4$ ounce)
unflavored gelatin
$1/4$ cup hot water
1 package (8 ounce) cream cheese,
softened
1 can ($10^3/4$ ounce) tomato soup
1 cup mayonnaise
Hot sauce to taste

Cayenne pepper to taste
Salt and pepper to taste
1 small purple onion, finely chopped
1 cup celery, chopped
$1/2$ green bell pepper, seeded and chopped
1 pound shrimp, peeled, cooked and chopped
2 ounces drained red caviar
Crackers or Melba toast

Dissolve gelatin in water. Whisk together cream cheese and next 4 ingredients. Season with salt and pepper. Add onion, celery, bell pepper and shrimp, combining well. Adjust seasoning if necessary. Line decorative mold with plastic wrap, then coat with nonstick cooking spray. Arrange caviar on bottom of mold, then carefully pour shrimp mixture into mold. Chill 12 to 24 hours. Invert onto serving plate and remove plastic wrap. Serve with assorted crackers or Melba toast. Yields 30-40 servings.

Easy and Delicious Crab Mold

note...

- Fresh crabmeat may be substituted with 1-2 cans (7 ounce) lump crabmeat. Rinse lump crabmeat in strainer and drain; refresh crabmeat by squeezing juice of half a small lemon over it.

- Crab Mold may also be served on a bed of lettuce and sliced tomato. May also be served as a hot appetizer in a chafing dish. Crab Mold will keep up to 5 days when chilled.

1	tablespoon unflavored gelatin
3	tablespoons water
1	can (10 ounce) cream of mushroom soup
2	packages (3 ounce) cream cheese, cubed
1	cup finely chopped celery
3	green onions, finely minced (including tops)

1   cup mayonnaise
8   ounces fresh crabmeat
Garlic powder to taste
Cayenne pepper to taste
2   teaspoons Worcestershire sauce
Freshly squeezed juice of ½ lemon
Melba toast, wheat or vegetable crackers

Stir gelatin into cool tap water and soften. Heat undiluted cream of mushroom soup slowly. Add gelatin mixture and stir. Add cream cheese, stirring over low heat until smooth. Add celery, green onions, mayonnaise and crabmeat; heat thoroughly, blending well. Add remaining ingredients to taste without overpowering delicate crab flavor. Pour into decorative mold greased with mayonnaise and chill overnight. Serve with Melba toast, wheat crackers or vegetable crackers. Yields 30-40 servings.

Provençal Goat Cheese Gratin

Lightly coat a shallow 10 to 12-inch gratin dish or six (6-inch) individual dishes with nonstick cooking spray.

Gratin:
Combine any mix of the following cheeses to make 1½ pounds. Transfer to prepared dish.
Goat Cheese, crumbled
Brie or Camembert, rind removed
Cream Cheese, softened
Gruyère, shredded
Monterey Jack, shredded
Gorgonzola, crumbled (sparingly)

Herb topping:
2   **teaspoons fresh rosemary, chopped and divided**
2   **teaspoons fresh oregano, chopped and divided**
2   **teaspoons fresh mint, chopped and divided (optional)**
1½ cups thick and chunky tomato sauce (your favorite)
24 black olives, pitted and chopped
Toast points or warm French bread

Combine rosemary, oregano and mint in small bowl. Sprinkle ½ of herb mixture over cheese. Spread tomato sauce over cheese. Sprinkle remaining herbs over sauce. Top with olives. Broil 3 to 5 minutes or until cheese is bubbly. Serve with toast points or warm French bread. Yields 10-12 servings.

note...
Fresh oregano may be substituted with 1 teaspoon dry oregano or herbes de Provence.

note...

This should only be made with flavorful summer tomatoes.

Summertime Tomato and Blue Cheese Spread

1   pound vine-ripened tomatoes, chopped
1   cup fresh chopped basil
3   garlic cloves, chopped
1   tablespoon extra virgin olive oil
1   pound blue cheese, Gorgonzola or Saga blue cheese
Melba rounds or toast points

Combine tomatoes, basil, garlic, oil and cheese, mixing gently. Keep at room temperature until ready to serve. Mound into glass bowl on serving tray and surround with melba rounds or toast points. Yields 20-25 servings.

Pesto and Sun-Dried Tomato Torte

1/2   cup Parmesan cheese, grated
1/4   cup shredded Romano cheese, grated
2   packages (8 ounce)
    cream cheese, softened
1/2   cup butter, softened
1/2   cup sour cream

1/2   cup minced sun-dried tomatoes, drained if oil-packed
1/2   cup pesto
4   ounces smoked salmon, chopped
Water crackers

Process cheeses, butter and sour cream in food processor 4-5 minutes on high speed. Lightly butter a small mold. Press sun-dried tomatoes into bottom of mold. Pour 1/3 of cheese mixture into mold. Arrange salmon slices on top. Pour 1/3 of cheese mixture over salmon. Spread pesto over cheese mixture. Pour remaining cheese mixture over pesto. Cover with plastic wrap and chill at least 3 hours in mold. Invert onto serving plate and serve with water crackers. Yields 20-25 servings.

Avocado Terrine

4   avocados, pitted, peeled and coarsely chopped
1   package (8 ounce) cream cheese, softened
1/2   teaspoon garlic salt
1   teaspoon chili powder
1/4   teaspoon cayenne pepper

3   tablespoons lemon juice
4   tomatoes, peeled, seeded and chopped
1/4   cup purple onion
1/2   cup sour cream
4   tablespoons fresh cilantro, chopped
Tortilla chips

Process avocados and cream cheese in food processor until just blended. Add garlic salt, chili powder, cayenne pepper and lemon juice and process until smooth. Remove mixture from processor and set aside. Place tomatoes and onion in bowl of clean food processor and pulse until finely chopped. Line loaf pan with plastic wrap and coat with nonstick cooking spray. Spoon 1/3 of avocado mixture into bottom of pan. Gently spread tomato mixture over avocado. Cover with 1/3 of avocado mixture. Spread sour cream over avocado layer. Spread remaining 1/3 of avocado mixture on top of sour cream. Cover with plastic wrap. Chill at least 8 hours. Before serving, remove plastic cover, then invert pan onto serving plate. Remove plastic wrap from mousse. Garnish with chopped cilantro. Serve with tortilla chips. Yields 16 servings.

Sun-Dried Tomatoes and Feta Terrine

1/2   cup butter, softened
12   ounces feta cheese
1   package (8 ounce) cream cheese, softened
2   garlic cloves, minced
4   dashes of hot sauce

1/2   cup toasted pine nuts
1   package (8 ounce) sun-dried tomatoes, minced and softened
1   cup pesto
Rosemary sprigs, for garnish
Crackers of choice

Process butter and next 4 ingredients in food processor. Line loaf pan with plastic wrap and coat plastic wrap with nonstick cooking spray. Layer pan with toasted pine nuts, sun-dried tomatoes and pesto. Top with cheese mixture. Bring plastic wrap over top of mixture and press gently; chill 4 hours. Invert pan onto serving plate; remove plastic wrap. Garnish with rosemary sprigs and serve with crackers. Yields 24 servings.

Fiesta Cheesecake

1½ cups finely crushed tortilla chips
¼ cup butter, melted
2 packages (8 ounce)
  cream cheese, softened
2 eggs
1 package (8 ounce)
  shredded pepper jack cheese
2 jalapeño peppers,
  seeded and chopped
1 can (4 ounce)
  chopped green chilies, drained
¼ teaspoon cayenne pepper

1 cup sour cream,
  at room temperature
1 green bell pepper, seeded and
  coarsely chopped
½ yellow bell pepper, seeded and
  coarsely chopped
½ red bell pepper, seeded and
  coarsely chopped
1 cup chopped green onions
1 large tomato, chopped
¼ cup black olives, sliced
Tortilla chips

Preheat oven to 350 degrees. Combine crushed tortilla chips and butter. Press tortilla mixture onto bottom of 9-inch springform pan and bake for 15 minutes. In medium bowl beat together cream cheese and eggs with electric mixer until well blended. Add cheese, jalapeños, green chilies and cayenne, mixing well. Pour this mixture over tortilla crust. Bake for 30 minutes. Set aside to cool. Spread sour cream over cooled cheesecake. Loosen rim by running a knife around edge and chill until ready to garnish. Garnish by making holiday or Southwestern design with bell peppers, green onions, tomatoes and olives. Use your imagination. Serve with tortilla chips. Yields 36-40 servings.

Confetti Bagel Bites

1 cup grated Monterey Jack cheese
¼ cup mayonnaise
2 tablespoons grated carrot
1 tablespoon chopped green onion
1 tablespoon seeded and finely chopped red bell pepper
1 package mini-bagels

note...
Substitute toasted bread, English muffins or small commercially prepared pizza rounds for mini-bagels.

Combine cheese and next 4 ingredients. Spread on each half of bagel. Broil until melted and bubbly. Cut into bite size wedges. Yields 4 servings per bagel.

Jalapeño Cheese Dip

1   **pound processed cheese product, cubed**
4   **ounces extra-sharp Cheddar cheese, grated**
1   **pint light mayonnaise**
8   **pickled or canned jalapeño peppers, seeded, peeled and chopped**
Juice from jalapeños to taste
1   **onion, finely chopped**
Tortilla chips

Bring cheeses to room temperature and process a small amount at a time in food processor, adding mayonnaise alternately with more cheese. Add jalapeños, juice to taste and onion; process until smooth. Chill until ready to serve. Serve with tortilla chips. Yields 24 servings.

Beef Queso Dip

$1\frac{1}{2}$ **pounds ground beef**
1   **onion, chopped**
2   **green onions, chopped**
2   **dried chilies, chopped**
1   **can ($10\frac{3}{4}$ ounce) tomato soup**
1   **can ($10\frac{3}{4}$ ounce) cream of mushroom soup**
2   **teaspoons chili powder**
1   **pound processed cheese product, cubed**
Tortilla or corn chips

In large skillet cook ground beef with onions, then drain. In large saucepan combine beef mixture with chilies, soups and chili powder. Simmer several hours. Add cheese, stirring until melted. Serve with tortilla chips or corn chips. Yields 50 servings.

Southwestern Poolside Dip

1 red onion, chopped
1 red bell pepper,
   seeded and chopped
1 yellow bell pepper,
   seeded and chopped
3-4 celery stalks, chopped
2 tomatoes, chopped
1 cup frozen corn,
   thawed and drained
½ cup fresh cilantro, chopped

2 jalapeño peppers, seeded and chopped
Juice of 1 lemon
1 tablespoon red wine vinegar
1 tablespoon cooking oil
Garlic salt to taste
Black pepper to taste
Cumin to taste
1 avocado, pitted and chopped
Juice of 1 lime
Tortilla chips

Combine onion and next 13 ingredients and chill overnight. Just before serving, toss avocado with lime juice and fold into mixture. Serve with tortilla chips. Yields 25-30 servings.

Tasty Corn and Green Chili Dip

1 carton (8 ounce) sour cream
1 cup mayonnaise
1 large can (15¼ ounce)
   whole kernel corn, drained
1 small can (8¾ ounce)
   whole kernel corn, drained

1 can (4½ ounce) chopped green chilies
½ cup grated Cheddar cheese
½ cup grated mozzarella cheese
Corn chips

Combine all ingredients together in serving bowl, tossing well. Serve with corn chips. Yields 25-30 servings.

Salsa Verde

4	green tomatoes, chopped	3	avocados, pitted and chopped
6	tomatillos, chopped	6	cilantro sprigs, chopped
2	jalapeños, seeded and chopped	1	teaspoon salt
3	garlic cloves, chopped	1½	cups sour cream

Combine tomatoes, tomatillos, jalapeños and garlic in saucepan. Bring to a boil, reduce heat and simmer 15 to 20 minutes; cool slightly. Place avocados, cilantro, salt and tomato mixture in food processor; purée until smooth. Add sour cream and pulse to combine well. Chill before serving. Yields about 4 cups.

Avocado Corn Guacamole

1	cup fresh corn kernels, 2-3 ears of corn	1	teaspoon chopped garlic
3	tablespoons cooking oil, divided	1	teaspoon cider vinegar
1	tomato, chopped	1½	teaspoons kosher salt
¼	cup fresh cilantro, chopped	¼	teaspoon cumin
2	tablespoons chopped red onion	2	avocados, chopped
1	teaspoon chopped jalapeño pepper	2	tablespoons fresh lime juice
			Tortilla chips

Preheat oven to 450 degrees. Cut kernels from cob. Roast corn kernels in 1 tablespoon oil about 7 to 8 minutes, stirring often. Let cool and place in medium bowl. Add 2 tablespoons oil and next 8 ingredients to corn, tossing gently. Cover and chill up to 6 hours. When ready to serve, toss avocados with lime juice; stir into corn mixture. Best when made shortly before serving. Serve with tortilla chips. Yields 10 servings.

note...
Keep guacamole from browning when prepared in advance by placing plastic wrap directly on the surface of the dip. It's oxygen that browns the avocado, so the less air that gets to the surface, the better. Store guacamole in the refrigerator until serving time.

Artichoke Chili Dip

3	garlic cloves, minced	1/2	cup mayonnaise
1	onion, coarsely chopped	1/4	teaspoon cayenne pepper
1-2	tablespoons olive oil	1	teaspoon dry mustard
2	cans (14 ounce) artichoke hearts, drained and coarsely chopped	1-1 1/2	cups grated Cheddar cheese
2	cans (4 1/2 ounce) chopped green chilies	1/4	cup seasoned breadcrumbs
			Tortilla chips or crackers

In large saucepan sauté garlic and onion in olive oil. Add artichokes and next 4 ingredients. Stir cheese into mixture. Transfer mixture to prepared casserole dish. Top with seasoned breadcrumbs; sprinkle lightly with additional cayenne and spray with nonstick cooking spray. Bake at 350 degrees for 15 to 20 minutes until bubbly. Serve with tortilla chips or crackers. Yields 2-3 cups.

Soups & Salads

Copper, Brass and Pewter
by John Cook

Notes...

- *To correct over-seasoning, add a raw, peeled and quartered potato and simmer for 15 minutes. Remove from the heat and discard the potato before serving.*
- *To remove fat from the top of soup, place a lettuce leaf in the stockpot. This will absorb the fat and can be removed easily.*
- *A large, heavy pot with a tight fitting lid may be used in place of a Dutch oven.*

Soups & Salads

Cream of Roasted Red Pepper Soup 42

Very Easy Tuscan White Bean Soup. 43

Tuscan Tomato Soup 43

Portobello Soup. 44

Absolutely Elegant Asparagus Soup 44

Holiday Curried Butternut Soup 45

Chunky Creamy Corn Chowder. 45

Roasted Lobster-Corn Chowder 46

Fresh Corn and Crab Bisque 47

Baked Potato Soup 47

Jalapeño-Potato Soup 48

Black-Eyed Pea Soup 48

Too Easy To Be Tortilla Soup 49

Southwestern Stew 50

Vegetable-Beef Stew 51

Beef Chili 52

White Chicken Chili 52

Spicy Cole Slaw 53

Super Simple Slaw 53

Incredible Croutons 54

Glazed Pecan Sprinkles for Salads 54

Bristol Style Salad Dressing. 54

French Café Salad 55

Texas Caesar Salad
with Cayenne Croutons 56

Wild Rice, Apricot and Almond Salad 57

Rice, Black Beans and Feta Salad 57

Cuban Rice and Black Bean Salad 58

Apple Cheese Nut Salad 58

Fresh Pear and Parmesan Salad 59

Fresh Fruit with Poppy Seed Dressing 60

Super Salad 61

Spicy Jicama Salad 62

Strawberry Spinach Salad 62

Marinated Shrimp, Mushroom
and Artichoke Salad. 63

Marinated Asparagus Salad 63

Warm Cabbage with Saga Blue Cheese 64

Cream of Roasted Red Pepper Soup

8	red bell peppers	1	teaspoon salt
6	garlic cloves, minced	½	teaspoon pepper
1	small onion, chopped	2	tablespoons all-purpose flour
3	tablespoons butter, divided	1½	cups heavy cream
2	cans (14 ounce) chicken broth		Fresh basil, cut into thin strips, for garnish
2	cups white wine		

Place peppers on an aluminum foil-lined baking sheet; broil 5 inches from heat about 5 minutes on each side or until peppers look blistered. Place roasted peppers in a heavy-duty, plastic freezer bag immediately; seal and let stand 10 minutes. Peel peppers; remove and discard stem and seeds. Set roasted peppers aside. Cook garlic and onion in 1 tablespoon butter in a Dutch oven over medium heat until tender. Add chicken broth, white wine, salt and pepper; bring to a boil. Reduce heat and simmer 30 minutes. Strain broth through a large wire mesh strainer into a large container. Reserve solids. Set broth mixture aside. In food processor bowl, add reserved solids and roasted peppers. Process 30 seconds or until mixture is smooth. Set pepper purée aside. Melt remaining 2 tablespoons butter in Dutch oven over low heat; add flour, stirring until smooth. Cook 1 minute, stirring constantly. Gradually add broth mixture to flour mixture; cook over medium heat, stirring constantly until thickened and bubbly (about 3 minutes). Stir in pepper puree. Gradually stir in cream. Cook over low heat until thoroughly heated. Garnish with basil. Yields 8, 1-cup servings.

Holiday Curried Butternut Soup

¼ cup unsalted butter
2 cups finely chopped
  yellow onions
6 teaspoons curry powder
2 medium butternut squash
  or 1 3-pound pumpkin

3½ cups chicken broth
2 apples, peeled, cored and chopped
1 cup apple juice
Salt and fresh ground pepper to taste
1 shredded, unpeeled tart apple, for garnish

In large saucepan melt butter. Add onions and curry powder. Cook covered over low heat until onions are tender (about 15 minutes). Peel squash or pumpkin, scrape out seeds and chop the flesh. When onions are tender, pour in broth, add squash or pumpkin and apples and bring to a boil. Reduce heat and simmer until squash and apples are very tender. Pour soup through a strainer, reserving liquid. Transfer solids to the bowl of a food processor. Add 1 cup stock to squash or pumpkin mixture and process until smooth. Return pureed soup to saucepan; add apple juice and remaining stock. Season to taste with salt and pepper and simmer briefly to thoroughly heat. Garnish with shredded apple and serve immediately. Yields 4-6 servings.

Chunky Creamy Corn Chowder

2 tablespoons diced bacon
½ cup diced onion
1 cup diced celery
3 tablespoons all-purpose flour
4 cups milk

1 can (17 ounce) cream style corn
1½ cups chopped, cooked potatoes
2 teaspoons salt
¼ teaspoon pepper
1 teaspoon Worcestershire sauce

Cook bacon in medium saucepan until brown. Add onion and celery; cook until tender. Blend in flour. Gradually add milk. Cook slowly until thickened, stirring constantly. Add corn and remaining ingredients; heat thoroughly. Yields 8 servings.

Roasted Lobster-Corn Chowder

note...

- *Two (1½ pound) steamed Maine lobsters will provide enough meat for this chowder.*

- *Frozen, cooked crawfish tails may be substituted for the lobster.*

2	tablespoons olive oil, divided	2	thyme sprigs
6	ears of corn	1	parsley sprig
1	cup finely chopped onion	1	bay leaf
1	cup finely chopped leek, washed well	2	cups coarsely chopped, cooked lobster meat
¾	cup finely chopped celery	2	cups evaporated milk
3	garlic cloves, minced	¾	teaspoon salt
¼	cup all-purpose flour	¼	teaspoon ground nutmeg
3-4	cans (10½ ounce) chicken broth	¼	teaspoon pepper
4	cups cubed red potatoes (about 1 pound)		Pinch of sugar
			Hot sauce to taste

Prepare grill or broiler. Brush 1 teaspoon oil over corn. Place corn on grill rack or broiler pan, and grill or broil 20 minutes or until corn is lightly browned, turning every 5 minutes; let cool. Reserving 2 cobs, cut kernels from cobs to measure 3 cups; set aside. Heat remaining oil in large Dutch oven over medium heat. Add onion, leek, celery and garlic; sauté 5 minutes or until tender. Sprinkle flour over onion mixture; cook 1 minute, stirring constantly. Add broth gradually, stirring with a wire whisk until well blended. Add reserved corncobs, potatoes, thyme, parsley and bay leaf; cover, reduce heat and simmer 5 minutes. Stir in corn kernels and milk; cover and simmer 10 minutes or until potatoes are tender. Remove and discard corncobs, thyme, parsley and bay leaf. Add lobster meat, salt and remaining ingredients; simmer, uncovered, 2 minutes. Top with dashes of hot sauce if desired. Yields 10-12 servings.

Too Easy To Be Tortilla Soup

1 onion, chopped
1 jalapeño pepper,
   chopped (optional)
4 garlic cloves, minced
2 tablespoons cooking oil
1 can (14½ ounce)
   chopped tomatoes
1 can (10 ounce)
   tomatoes with chilies
2 cans (14½ ounce) low salt
   chicken broth
1 can (10¾ ounce) tomato soup
1½ soup cans water

1 teaspoon ground cumin
1 teaspoon chili powder
1 teaspoon salt
½ teaspoon lemon pepper
1 teaspoon Worcestershire sauce
½ teaspoon hot sauce
4 chicken breasts, cooked and
   cut into bite-size pieces, or shredded
4 tortillas, cut in strips, for garnish
Shredded Cheddar cheese, for garnish
Chopped avocado, for garnish
Chopped cilantro, for garnish
Lime wedges to squeeze, if desired

note...

For crispy tortilla chips, place sliced tortillas on baking sheet. Spray with cooking spray. Bake in a 475 degree oven until crisp. Lightly salt if desired. Use in recipe for garnish.

Sauté onion, jalapeño pepper and garlic in oil until tender and golden. Puree both cans tomatoes and set aside. In a large Dutch oven, combine chicken broth and next 8 ingredients. Add sautéed onion mixture, pureed tomatoes and chopped chicken. Cover and simmer 1 hour. Garnish with tortilla strips, cheddar cheese, avocado and cilantro. Tortilla Soup will freeze well. Yields 8-10 servings.

Southwestern Stew

1½ cups unbleached, all-purpose flour

1 tablespoon dried thyme

1½ teaspoons salt

½ teaspoon freshly ground black pepper

3 pounds beef stew meat, cut in 1-inch cubes

¼ cup olive oil

1 cup dry red wine

1½ cups beef broth, canned, fresh or frozen

1½ cups canned crushed tomatoes

2 tablespoons ground cumin

2 teaspoons chili powder

6 garlic cloves, chopped

1 bay leaf

8-12 frozen white pearl onions

½ cup chopped Italian parsley

1½ cups green Sicilian olives

Preheat oven to 350 degrees. Combine flour, thyme, salt and pepper in a plastic freezer bag. Add beef cubes a little at a time and shake. Transfer to a plate and discard flour. Heat oil in Dutch oven. Add beef cubes in batches to brown on all sides. Transfer to paper towels to drain. Discard remaining oil. Add wine, beef broth and tomatoes to Dutch oven. Bring to a boil and stir to remove browned bits from bottom of pan. Return beef to Dutch oven. Add cumin, chili powder, garlic, bay leaf and additional salt and pepper to taste. Bake for 1 hour, 30 minutes. Thaw pearl onions, add after baking. Cook, uncovered, 15 minutes. Add parsley and olives. Cook until beef is tender (about 15 minutes). Yields 6 servings.

Vegetable-Beef Stew

1	large chuck roast	1	can (15¼ ounce)
2	cans (14½ ounce)		whole kernel corn
	stewed tomatoes	2	cups chopped carrots
3	cans (14½ ounce) chicken broth,	1	head of cabbage, chopped
	or more if needed	1	can (14½ ounce) green beans
1	onion, chopped	4	cups fresh or frozen peas
1	bunch celery, chopped	2	potatoes, peeled and cubed
	Salt and pepper	1	package (12 ounce) macaroni,
	Seasoned salt		cooked according to package directions
	Lemon pepper		

In Dutch oven brown roast on all sides. Add tomatoes and next 6 ingredients. Cover and simmer 2 to 3 hours. Add corn and next 5 ingredients. More broth may need to be added if stew is too thick. Add as desired. Place ⅓ cup cooked macaroni in bottom of each serving bowl before ladling in stew. Yields 8-10 servings.

Beef Chili

note...

- *Thaw frozen chili in refrigerator overnight. Reheat over medium heat.*

1	**pound lean ground beef**
1	**onion, chopped**
1	**teaspoon seasoning salt**
1	**teaspoon garlic salt**
1-2	**teaspoons chili powder**
1/4	**teaspoon cayenne pepper**
1	**bay leaf**
1	**teaspoon Worcestershire sauce**
2	**cans (8 ounce) tomato sauce**
1	**can (16 ounce) kidney beans, drained and rinsed**
1	**teaspoon cumin**

Brown beef and pour off fat. Combine ingredients in a crockpot on low heat. Cover and cook in crockpot on high 2-3 hours or on low 5-6 hours. Remove bay leaf before serving. Yields 6-8 servings.

White Chicken Chili

- *For a great substitute and time saver, skin, bone and shred your favorite fully cooked rotisserie chicken.*

1	**tablespoon olive oil**
1	**pound skinned, boned chicken breast, diced**
1/2	**cup shallots, chopped**
5	**garlic cloves, minced**
2	**cans (11 ounce) tomatillos, drained and coarsely chopped**
1	**can (14 1/2 ounce) whole tomatoes, undrained and coarsely chopped**
1	**can (14 1/4 ounce) chicken broth**
1	**can (4 1/2 ounce) chopped green chilies**
1/2	**teaspoon dried oregano**
1/2	**teaspoon coriander seeds, crushed**
1	**teaspoon ground cumin**
2	**cans (16 ounce) cannellini beans or other white beans, drained and rinsed**
3	**tablespoons fresh lime juice**
1/4	**teaspoon pepper**
6	**tablespoons shredded sharp Cheddar or Monterey Jack cheese**

Salt and pepper to taste

Heat oil in a saucepan coated with cooking spray over medium heat until hot. Add chicken and sauté 3 minutes or until done. Remove from pan and set aside. Add shallots and garlic to pan and sauté until tender. Stir in tomatillos and next 6 ingredients; bring to a boil. Reduce heat and simmer 20 minutes. Add chicken and beans; cook 5 minutes or until thoroughly heated. Stir in lime juice and pepper. Top with cheese. Yield 8-10 servings.

French Café Salad

Dressing:

1   tablespoon freshly squeezed lemon or lime juice
1   garlic clove, crushed
1   shallot, minced
2   tablespoons sugar
Sea salt to taste
4   tablespoons walnut oil or extra virgin olive oil
Freshly ground black pepper to taste

In large, shallow salad bowl, whisk together lemon or lime juice and next 4 ingredients. Whisk in oil and pepper.

Salad:

1   firm ripe pear, at room temperature
4   heads of Belgian endive, rinsed and trimmed
2½ ounces Roquefort cheese
½   cup walnuts, halved, toasted and chopped
3   tablespoons fresh chives, finely snipped
½   cup fresh blueberries
Pepper to taste

Peel, core and cut pear into 16 lengthwise slices. Add to dressing, tossing gently to coat and set aside. Separate endive leaves, but do not cut or tear. Add endive, Roquefort, walnuts, chives and blueberries to salad bowl. Toss ingredients, coating thoroughly with dressing. Season with pepper and arrange on individual salad plates. Yields 4 servings.

note...

For a beautiful presentation, place endive leaves in a daisy pattern on the salad plates. Top with remaining ingredients and serve.

Texas Caesar Salad with Cayenne Croutons

note...

Croutons may be made one day ahead and stored in an airtight container.

Dressing:

3   garlic cloves, peeled

2   shallots, peeled

2   anchovies

2   fresh jalapeños, seeded

1   bunch cilantro, coarsely chopped

1/2   cup red wine vinegar

1/2   cup shredded Romano cheese

1   egg yolk

1/2   teaspoon cracked black pepper

1   teaspoon lemon juice

Salt to taste

1   cup olive oil

Place garlic and next 10 ingredients in blender or food processor and puree. Add olive oil, blending until smooth, and chill.

Cayenne Croutons:

1/2   loaf white bread,
      cut into 1/2-inch cubes

1/3   cup melted unsalted butter

1   teaspoon chili powder

1/2   teaspoon cayenne pepper

1/3   teaspoon cumin

1/4   teaspoon salt

Preheat oven to 350 degrees. Place bread cubes in large bowl and toss with butter and remaining ingredients, coating well. Spread bread cubes in single layer on baking sheet. Bake until crisp and golden brown, stirring occasionally. Transfer croutons to wire rack and cool thoroughly before adding to salad.

Salad:

1   head of romaine lettuce

1   red bell pepper

1   yellow bell pepper

1   can (8 3/4 ounce)
    whole kernel corn, drained

1   teaspoon olive oil

1/4   cup sun-dried tomatoes, sliced thin

1/4   cup shredded Romano cheese

Wash lettuce, pat dry and cut into bite-size pieces. Chill lettuce to crisp. Place peppers on an aluminum foil-lined baking sheet; broil 5 inches from heat about 5 minutes on each side or until peppers look blistered. Place roasted peppers in plastic freezer bag immediately; seal and let stand 10 minutes. Peel peppers; remove and discard stem and seeds. Cut peppers into strips and set aside. Sauté corn kernels in oil over medium heat until tender. Drain and cool. In large bowl combine lettuce and dressing, tossing well. Add croutons and toss again. Serve in chilled bowls; garnish with pepper strips, corn, sun-dried tomatoes and Romano cheese. Yields 6-8 servings.

Wild Rice, Apricot and Almond Salad

5   cups chicken broth
2   cups wild rice, rinsed
1   cup dried apricots,
    coarsely chopped
1/2 cup dried currants
1   cup slivered almonds, toasted
2/3 cup chopped red onion

1/2 cup chopped fresh parsley
6   tablespoons tarragon vinegar
4   teaspoons Dijon mustard
2   garlic cloves, minced
3/4 cup olive oil
Salt and pepper to taste

Bring chicken broth to a boil in large, heavy saucepan. Mix in wild rice. Reduce heat to low. Simmer, uncovered, until rice is just tender, stirring occasionally. Drain rice well and transfer to large bowl. Mix dried apricots and currants into rice mixture and cool completely. Mix toasted almonds, chopped red onion and parsley into rice and set aside. Whisk tarragon vinegar, Dijon mustard and minced garlic in small bowl. Gradually whisk in olive oil. Mix just enough dressing into salad to moisten well. Season with salt and pepper. Salad may be prepared up to 8 hours in advance. Best served at room temperature. Yields 8 servings.

Rice, Black Beans and Feta Salad

1   can (15 ounce) black beans, rinsed and drained
1 1/2 cups chopped fresh tomatoes
1 1/2 cups cooked rice, cooled
1   package (4 ounce) crumbled feta cheese
1/2 cup chopped celery
1/2 cup chopped green onions
2   tablespoons chopped fresh parsley
1/2 cup Italian dressing

Combine all ingredients, tossing well to coat, and chill until ready to serve. Yields 6-8 servings.

Cuban Rice and Black Bean Salad

4	boneless, skinless chicken breasts		1/4	cup cilantro, chopped
2	cans (16 ounce) black beans, rinsed and drained		1/3	cup peanut oil
1	green bell pepper, seeded and chopped		1/3	cup fresh lime juice (about 3 limes)
1	red bell pepper, seeded and chopped		1	tablespoon garlic, minced
4	green onions, chopped		3	cups cooked white rice
				Seasoned salt
				Freshly ground black pepper

Grill chicken breasts and cut into 1/4-inch pieces. Combine chicken and next 9 ingredients in large bowl and mix thoroughly. Add salt and ground pepper to taste. Chill until ready to serve. Yields 8 servings.

Apple Cheese Nut Salad

Dressing:

1/2	cup apple juice		1/2	teaspoon salt
1/4	cup apple cider vinegar		1	shallot, minced
2-3	tablespoons sugar, or to taste		1/3-1/2	cup olive oil, more for a thicker dressing
2	tablespoons Dijon mustard			

Process apple juice and next 5 ingredients in food processor. Pour olive oil into processor in a steady stream until well blended.

Salad:

8   cups romaine or mixed lettuce, washed and torn
3/4 cup blue or feta cheese (about 3 ounces)
1/3 cup chopped walnuts or pecans, toasted
2   sliced golden delicious apples

Combine salad ingredients in large bowl. Toss with dressing just before serving. Yields 4-6 servings.

Fresh Pear and Parmesan Salad

Dressing:

1   shallot, minced

2   garlic cloves, minced

2-3 tablespoons sugar, or to taste

1-2 tablespoons water, optional

1   cup extra virgin olive oil

½   teaspoon kosher salt

Juice of 1 large lime

Pepper

Place dressing ingredients in food processor and pulse until well blended. Add water if dressing is too tart.

Salad:

2   bunches endive, sliced

3   cups coarsely torn romaine or Bibb lettuce

1   small head of radicchio, leaves separated

1½ cups sliced fresh fennel bulb, cored and sliced thin

3   tablespoons pine nuts, toasted

2   ripe Bosc pears, peeled, cored and thinly sliced

1   cup shaved Parmesan cheese

Toss endive, lettuce, radicchio and fennel together in large salad bowl. Add pine nuts, pears and Parmesan to greens. Toss with enough dressing to coat. Serve immediately. Yields 6 servings.

note...
To prevent browning, slice and add pears just before serving.

Fresh Fruit with Poppy Seed Dressing

Poppy Seed Dressing:

1½ cups sugar

2   teaspoons dry mustard

2   teaspoons salt

⅔   cup vinegar

3   tablespoons onion juice

2   cups cooking oil

3   tablespoons poppy seeds

Combine sugar, mustard, salt and vinegar in mixing bowl. Purée onion in food processor and add to mixing bowl. Beat on medium speed with an electric mixer. Slowly drizzle in oil. Beat until thickened. Add poppy seeds and beat for 1 minute. Chill until ready to serve.

Salad:

1   fresh pineapple, cubed

1   cantaloupe, cubed

½   honeydew, cubed

2   oranges, peeled and cut into bite size pieces

20-25 red seedless grapes, halved

2   pears, peeled and cut into bite size pieces

2   apples, peeled and cut into bite size pieces

Combine fruits in large bowl and gently toss. Top individual salads with dressing. Yields 8-10 servings.

note...

Add pears and apples to fruit mixture just before serving in order to avoid discoloration.

Super Salad

Dressing:

¾ **cup oil**
¼ **cup white wine vinegar**
½ **teaspoon salt**
¼ **teaspoon sugar**
¼ **teaspoon pepper**

Combine dressing ingredients in mixing bowl, blending well.

Salad:

1 **can (6 or 14 ounce) artichoke hearts, quartered**
2 **cups frozen peas**
1 **purple onion, sliced**
½ **pound fresh spinach, washed and stemmed**
1 **head of Bibb lettuce**
1 **head of iceberg lettuce**
2 **avocados, sliced**
1 **can (11 ounce) Mandarin oranges, drained**
½ **cup blue cheese, crumbled**

Marinate artichoke hearts, peas and onion slices in dressing at least 2 hours. Combine greens, avocados, oranges and blue cheese in large salad bowl. Pour dressing mixture over greens, tossing well. Yields 6 servings.

Spicy Jicama Salad

1 **pound jicama, peeled and julienned**	1 **red apple, cored and julienned**
Juice of 1 orange	3 **tangerines, peel and pith removed, cut into segments and halved**
Juice of 1 lime	1/4 **cup chopped cilantro or more to taste**
Juice of 1/2 grapefruit	1/2 **small arbol chile, stemmed, seeded and ground to a powder**
1/4 **teaspoon salt**	
1/4 **cup olive oil**	6 **leaves romaine lettuce**

In a large non-reactive bowl, combine jicama with juices and salt. Toss to mix, cover and allow to set at room temperature for 1 hour. About 15 minutes before serving, add olive oil, apple sticks, tangerine segments and cilantro. Toss gently every few minutes until serving time. Season with ground chile and toss again before serving. Scoop generous portion into each romaine leaf. Serve immediately. Yields 6 servings.

Strawberry Spinach Salad

Dressing:

3 **tablespoons raspberry vinegar**	2/3 **cup sugar**
2 **tablespoons honey mustard**	1/2 **cup olive oil**
2 **tablespoons white wine**	1/2 **cup cooking oil**
2 **tablespoons lemon juice**	3 **tablespoons raspberry liqueur**
3 **tablespoons poppy seeds**	

Whisk vinegar, mustard and wine together in small bowl. Add lemon juice and poppy seeds and whisk well. Whisk in sugar, oils and liqueur.

Salad:

1 **package fresh spinach, washed and torn**
25 **fresh strawberries, capped and sliced**
1 **purple onion, sliced**
1/3 **cup pecans, toasted**

Combine salad ingredients in large bowl. Pour dressing over salad and gently toss. Yields 6 servings.

Marinated Shrimp, Mushroom and Artichoke Salad

1   package (1 ounce) Blue cheese flavored dry salad dressing mix
1   package (1 ounce) Italian flavored dry salad dressing mix
1   package (1 ounce) Garlic flavored dry salad dressing mix
1/2 teaspoon salt
2-3 pounds fresh shrimp, cooked and peeled
1   jar (2 1/4 ounce) capers, rinsed and drained
2-3 onions, thinly sliced into rings
2   cans (4 ounce) whole button mushrooms, drained
2   cans (14 ounce) tiny artichoke hearts, drained

Prepare salad dressings according to package directions, omitting water and replacing with vinegar. (Slightly less oil may be used.) Add salt to dressing, combining well. Marinate shrimp and remaining ingredients in dressing overnight. Stir occasionally, avoiding breaking artichoke hearts. Serve on individual salad plates. Yields 10-12 servings.

note...
Leftover salad is delicious served over your favorite pasta, topped with Parmesan cheese.

Marinated Asparagus Salad

Dressing:

1/2 cup lemon juice	2 teaspoons Dijon mustard
1/4 cup olive oil	1/2 teaspoon basil
1/8 cup red wine vinegar	1 teaspoon salt
2 garlic cloves, minced	4 teaspoons pepper

Whisk together dressing ingredients, blending well.

Salad:

30 asparagus stems, cut into bite size pieces	3 tomatoes, cut into wedges
	2 purple onions, cut into rings

Combine salad ingredients in large bowl. Pour dressing over vegetables. Let chill at least 2 hours before serving. Yields 6 servings.

Warm Cabbage with Saga Blue Cheese

6   ounces bacon, chopped
Freshly ground black pepper
2   **shallots, minced**
1   **cup white wine**
1½ cups heavy cream
1   **tablespoon Bovril (or reduced beef stock concentrate)**
1   **tablespoon Dijon mustard**
1   **head of cabbage, sliced**
2   **tablespoons white vinegar**
6   **ounces crumbled Saga blue cheese**

Cook diced bacon in large skillet and season with pepper. Drain bacon on paper towel and set aside; reserve bacon drippings. In saucepan combine shallot, wine and 1 teaspoon pepper. Cook until almost evaporated. Add cream, reduced beef stock concentrate and mustard, stirring occasionally. Cook on medium heat until thickened. (Bacon and cream mixture may be prepared ahead and reheated.) Heat reserved drippings in large skillet; add cabbage and toss 1 minute. Add vinegar and toss 1 minute. Add cream mixture and blue cheese, tossing well to combine. Divide evenly among 6 plates and sprinkle with bacon. Yields 6 servings.

Under the Bridge
by John Cook

Notes...

- *Deglazing refers to heating stock, wine or any type of liquid in the pan, in which the meat or seafood has been cooked, mixing with the pan juices and sediment to form a gravy or sauce base.*
- *Always allow a roasted piece of meat to rest for 10 to 15 minutes before carving. This resting time allows the juices to retreat back into the meat.*
- *Marinate in the refrigerator, never at room temperature.*

Meat & Poultry

Beef Fillet Steaks with
Mushrooms and Béarnaise Sauce 66

Roast Tenderloin of Beef
with Madeira Sauce 67

Beef Tenderloin with Mushrooms 68

Party Buffet Marinated Beef Tenderloin 69

Beef Tenderloin Steaks
with Peppercorn Sauce 70

Super Easy Baby Back Ribs 70

Super Easy Beef Brisket 71

Rack of Veal with
Garlic and Rosemary 72

Veal Cutlets in Mustard Cream Sauce 72

Spicy Family Night Meatloaf 73

Sweet and Savory
Marinated Pork Tenderloin 74

Sherry Marinated Pork Tenderloin 74

Grilled Honey Glazed Pork Tenderloin 75

Pork Tenderloin with Raspberry Sauce 76

Honey-Sage Pork Tenderloin 77

Spicy Pork Tenderloin
with Lime Mayonnaise 78

Peppered Pork Tenderloin 79

Eastern North Carolina Pork Barbecue 79

Best Baby Back Ribs 80

Western Style Baby Back Ribs 80

Pork Chops Victoria 81

Smothered Pork Loin Chops 81

Barbecued Lamb Chops
with Plum-Mint Sauce 82

Grilled Apricot Lamb Chops 83

Charcoaled Leg of Lamb 83

Spinach Chicken Crêpes 84

Chicken Smothered with Onions 85

Herb Roasted Chicken Breasts 85

Chicken Breasts with
Garlic Balsamic Vinegar Sauce 86

Super Easy Crispy Chicken 86

Italian Chicken 87

Garlic Sour Cream Chicken 87

Chicken with Spicy Peanut Sauce 88

Chicken Dijonnaise 89

Chicken in Roquefort Sauce 89

Curry Chicken with
Tomatoes and Raisins 90

Easy Hawaiian Chicken 90

Mediterranean Chicken 91

French Bistro Grilled Chicken 91

Creamy Poblano Chicken
with Cornbread Waffles 92

Pasilla Chicken Enchiladas 93

Salsa Chicken Enchiladas 94

Tequila Chicken with Citrus Salsa 95

Glazed Cornish Hens
with Savory Stuffing 96

Game Day Turkey Tailgate Sandwich 96

Beef Fillet Steaks with Mushrooms and Béarnaise Sauce

2 tablespoons unsalted butter	1½ teaspoons tomato paste
4 large shallots, minced	1 tablespoon cooking oil
¾ pound mushrooms, finely chopped	6 center cut fillet steaks (tournedos), 1-inch thick
¼ teaspoon salt	Béarnaise Sauce
⅛ teaspoon freshly ground black pepper	Watercress sprigs, for garnish

In large heavy skillet melt butter over moderate heat. Add shallots and cook until tender, but not browned (about 2 minutes). Increase heat to moderately high and stir in mushrooms. Sauté until most of moisture has evaporated (about 4 minutes). Season with salt and pepper. Remove from heat and stir in tomato paste. (Mushrooms may be prepared up to 3 hours in advance. Set aside at room temperature.) In large heavy skillet heat oil over moderately high heat. Add steaks and sauté, turning, until rare or medium-rare, 3 to 4 minutes on each side. Season with additional salt and pepper to taste. Top each steak with mushrooms and warm Béarnaise Sauce. Garnish with watercress sprigs. Serve remaining sauce separately. Yields 6 servings.

Béarnaise Sauce:

¾ cup unsalted butter	2 tablespoons tarragon vinegar
2 shallots, finely chopped	2 tablespoons dry white wine
1 teaspoon dried tarragon	2 egg yolks
1 teaspoon dried chervil	2 tablespoons water
¼ teaspoon freshly ground black pepper	Salt to taste

In small saucepan warm butter over low heat, being careful not to burn; set aside. In small, heavy nonmetal saucepan, combine shallots and next 5 ingredients. Boil over moderately high heat until liquid is reduced to 1 teaspoon (about 2 minutes). Add egg yolks and 2 tablespoons water to reduction, whisking constantly over moderate heat until thickened and fluffy (about 2 to 3 minutes); remove from heat. Continue whisking several seconds. Sauce should be thick enough to cling to whisk. Let cool 3 minutes before slowly adding melted butter. Whisk continually while adding butter. Season with salt to taste. Keep sauce warm in double boiler over warm water up to 1 hour before serving.

Party Buffet Marinated Beef Tenderloin

note...
Serve with Dijon mustard or home-made mayonnaise.

1   (3 pound) beef tenderloin
2   teaspoons cooking oil
2/3 cup balsamic vinegar
2   teaspoons salt
2   teaspoons water-packed
    canned or freeze-dried
    green peppercorns, crushed
4   tablespoons chives,
    finely chopped
2   teaspoons fresh tarragon or
    1/2 teaspoon dried tarragon

2   teaspoons fresh thyme or
    1/2 teaspoon dried thyme
2   garlic cloves, minced
2   teaspoons Dijon mustard
1 1/3 cups extra virgin olive oil
2   whole roasted red peppers
    (inside membrane removed), finely diced
2   celery stalks, thinly sliced
2   purple onions, thinly sliced
Red-tipped lettuce, for garnish
Cherry or pear-shaped tomatoes, for garnish

Preheat oven to 475 degrees. Roll tenderloin and tie securely with cooking twine. Place in roasting pan; transfer to oven and immediately reduce heat to 375 degrees. Roast 35-45 minutes or until meat thermometer inserted in middle is 130 degrees for rare. Remove from pan and place on rack to cool to room temperature. Combine vinegar and next 7 ingredients, blending until salt dissolves. Stir in olive oil and blend well. Pour over roasted peppers, celery and onions and set aside. Remove twine from cooled meat. Slice as thinly as possible, no thicker than 1/4-inch, placing the pieces back together in tenderloin shape. Place in long, narrow and deep container and cover with vegetables and dressing. Allow to marinate several hours. It may be chilled overnight, then removed the next day and allowed to return to room temperature before serving. Just before serving, arrange lettuce leaves on large serving tray. Arrange reassembled tenderloin in center. Garnish with tomatoes. Meat should be perfectly cooked, pink in center, but not overly rare. Yields 4-6 servings.

Beef Tenderloin Steaks with Peppercorn Sauce

2   tablespoons unsalted butter
¼   cup chopped shallots
⅓   cup brandy
1   cup beef broth
1   cup crème fraîche or heavy cream

Salt to taste
1   tablespoon four peppercorn blend, coarsely ground
8   (6 ounce) beef tenderloin steaks
¼   cup cooking oil

Melt butter in heavy, medium saucepan over medium heat. Add shallots and sauté until golden (about 8 minutes). Add brandy and bring to boil. Add broth and boil until reduced to 1 cup (about 5 minutes). Add crème fraîche or heavy cream and peppercorns. Cook over medium heat until reduced to sauce consistency (about 3 minutes if using crème fraîche or 8 minutes if using cream). Season with salt. Preheat grill. Brush steaks with oil. Season with salt and pepper. Grill to desired doneness. Bring sauce to a simmer. Transfer steaks to serving plates. Spoon sauce over steaks. Serve with remaining sauce on the side. Yields 6 servings.

Super Easy Baby Back Ribs

note...
Ribs may be pre-cooked a day in advance and chilled until ready to grill.

4   pounds baby back ribs
Salt and pepper to taste
Paprika
¾   cup ketchup
¼   cup brown sugar
2   tablespoons cider vinegar
1   teaspoon chili powder

Place ribs bone side down in shallow roasting pan. Season generously with salt, pepper, and paprika. Bake at 350 degrees for 1 hour. In bowl combine ketchup, brown sugar, vinegar and chili powder, mixing well. Place cooked ribs bone side down on grill over medium heat. Cook 20 minutes or until thoroughly heated. Brush occasionally with sauce. Do not turn ribs. Yields 4-6 servings.

Super Easy Beef Brisket

1   (5-6 pound) brisket
Garlic powder, shake to lightly cover
Worcestershire sauce, shake to lightly cover
Seasoned salt, shake to lightly cover
¼   cup Liquid Smoke
Kosher salt and pepper to taste

Cover brisket in garlic powder, Worcestershire sauce, seasoned salt and Liquid Smoke. Rub onto meat. Sprinkle with Kosher salt and pepper. Bake at 450 degrees for 30 minutes, uncovered, then wrap tightly in aluminum foil. Bake at 225 degrees for 5 to 6 hours. Remove from oven and slice meat. Reserve pan drippings. Remove excess fat from drippings. Yields 6-8 servings.

Gravy:
⅓   cup Worcestershire sauce
1   cup ketchup
¾   cup brown sugar
2   tablespoons lemon juice

Combine ingredients in small bowl, mixing well. Add reserved drippings. Pour over sliced brisket and bake at 225 degrees, uncovered, for 30 additional minutes.

Rack of Veal with Garlic and Rosemary

3/4	cup unsalted butter, at room temperature	1	teaspoon salt
8	garlic cloves, peeled	1	teaspoon freshly ground black pepper
1/3	cup fresh rosemary leaves or 5 teaspoons dried rosemary, crushed	1	(4 pound) rack of veal (6 ribs)
		1	cup chicken or veal broth
			Rosemary sprigs
2	tablespoons minced parsley		Lemon slices, for garnish

Preheat oven to 350 degrees. In food processor combine butter and next 5 ingredients; process until smooth. Rub butter mixture over veal. Place veal in roasting pan. Bake in lower third of oven for 1 hour, 15 minutes, to 1 hour, 30 minutes, or until meat thermometer registers 130 degrees. Let veal stand 15 minutes. Transfer to serving platter. Add broth to roasting pan and bring to a boil on top of stove. Stir vigorously, scraping brown bits. Strain into gravy boat. Slice veal and garnish with rosemary and lemon slices. Yields 6 servings.

Veal Cutlets in Mustard Cream Sauce

1/4	cup butter	2/3	cup white wine
3	tablespoons oil	1/3	cup coarse-grain Dijon mustard
8	green onions, chopped	2	cups heavy cream
4	large veal cutlets	1	large tomato, chopped
	Salt and pepper to taste		

Flatten veal cutlets between 2 sheets of plastic wrap until 1/4 inch thick. Melt butter and oil together in large skillet; add green onions and sauté. Raise the heat to medium-high. Season veal with salt and pepper to taste. Add veal to skillet and cook 1 minute on each side, being careful not to overcook. Remove from skillet and keep warm. Add wine to skillet and bring to a boil; cook until reduced. Whisk in mustard and heavy cream; boil 2 minutes. Adjust seasonings if needed. Place veal on serving plate and top with sauce. Sprinkle chopped tomato over veal and serve immediately. Serve with pasta or potatoes. Yields 4 servings.

Spicy Family Night Meatloaf

12	crackers, crushed	1	onion, chopped
1	can (6 ounce) spicy vegetable juice	1/4	cup egg substitute or 1 large egg
1	pound ground turkey or chicken breast		Garlic salt to taste
1	green bell pepper, seeded and chopped		Black pepper
		1	package (1.25 ounce) onion soup mix

Sauce:
1/2   cup honey
1/4   cup mustard
1   can (6 ounce) spicy vegetable juice

Preheat oven to 350 degrees. In small bowl soak crackers in juice. In large bowl combine crackers, ground turkey and next 6 ingredients, mixing well. Transfer to greased loaf pan. Combine honey, mustard and juice and pour over meatloaf. Bake for 1 hour. Yields 6 servings.

Sweet and Savory Marinated Pork Tenderloin

1	can (12 ounce) pineapple juice	1	teaspoon salt
½	cup olive oil	3	teaspoons black pepper
3	tablespoons Worcestershire sauce	3	garlic cloves, minced
2	teaspoons dry mustard		Thyme to taste
		2	pork tenderloins

Combine pineapple juice and next 7 ingredients. Pour over tenderloins and chill at least 3 hours. Preheat oven to 350 degrees. Bake for 20-30 minutes, internal temperature 150-160 degrees. Yields 4-6 servings.

note...

- *Tenderloins may also be grilled. Cook tenders over low heat 30 to 40 minutes, basting several times.*

Sherry Marinated Pork Tenderloin

¼ cup soy sauce
½ cup dry sherry
3 garlic cloves, crushed
2 tablespoons dry mustard
1½ teaspoons ground ginger
1 teaspoon dried thyme
2 pounds pork tenderloins

Combine soy sauce and next 5 ingredients in small bowl, mixing well. Place pork in large plastic zip-top bag. Pour marinade into bag and chill overnight. Transfer pork and marinade to casserole dish; bring to room temperature. Bake at 350 degrees for 20 to 30 minutes, basting occasionally. Pork is ready when meat thermometer inserted into thickest portion registers 150-160 degrees. Do not overcook. (Meat will continue to cook while resting.) Yields 4-6 servings.

note...

- *For buffet preparation, slice pork ahead, baste generously with marinade and cover with foil for up to an hour. Partially slice dinner rolls. Place in foil lined tray and warm in oven; remove from oven and cover with foil to keep moist. Rolls may be heated and transferred easily to serving tray for sliced pork sandwiches.*

Grilled Honey Glazed Pork Tenderloin

2   (1 pound) pork tenderloins, trimmed
2   tablespoons minced fresh parsley
2   tablespoons minced fresh or 2 teaspoons dried oregano
1½ teaspoons minced fresh or ½ teaspoon dried rosemary
1½ teaspoons minced fresh or ½ teaspoon dried thyme
1   tablespoon minced garlic
1   tablespoon beef bouillon granules, optional
1½ teaspoons salt
1½ teaspoons freshly ground black pepper

Spray grill rack with nonstick cooking spray and prepare grill for medium to low indirect heat by spreading coals from center and placing drip pan under rack. Rinse tenderloins under cold, running water and pat dry. Combine parsley and remaining ingredients and rub over tenderloins and let stand at room temperature 30 minutes. Place tenderloins on grill directly over fire and sear briefly on all sides. Position meat over drip pan; cover grill. Roast tenderloins over low indirect heat, turning every 10 to 15 minutes and brushing with Honey Mustard Glaze. Remove from grill when meat thermometer inserted into the thickest portion of meat registers between 140 and 145 degrees (about 45 minutes to 1 hour). Slice crosswise into medallions about ¼-inch thick. Yields 4-6 servings.

Honey Mustard Glaze:
2   tablespoons coarse-grained Dijon mustard
2   tablespoons firmly packed brown sugar
5   tablespoons honey

Combine ingredients in sauce pan and simmer over low heat until sugar melts (about 5 minutes).

note...
- Spices may be minced together in a small food processor.

- Instead of grilling, place in broiler; quickly sear then bake in oven at 375 degrees for 20-30 minutes.

Pork Tenderloin with Raspberry Sauce

2   (1 pound) pork tenderloins
1/4   cup soy sauce
1/4   cup olive oil
2   teaspoons minced garlic
2   teaspoons minced shallots
1   teaspoon black pepper

Combine soy sauce and next 4 ingredients in small bowl, mixing well. Place tenderloins in large zip-top plastic bag and pour marinade into bag. Seal and chill 24 hours. Preheat grill to medium heat. Spray grill rack with nonstick cooking spray. Remove tenderloins from marinade and transfer to grill. Grill tenderloins, basting with remaining marinade, until meat thermometer inserted into thickest portion registers 150-160 degrees. Serve hot or at room temperature with Raspberry Sauce on the side. Yields 4-6 servings.

Raspberry Sauce:
2   tablespoons shallots, chopped
1   tablespoon olive oil
1   cup Merlot
1   jar (8 ounce) seedless raspberry jelly
1   tablespoon arrowroot

In small saucepan sauté shallots in olive oil. Add Merlot and bring to a simmer. Add jelly, stirring until jelly melts. Combine arrowroot with small amount of water, mixing well. Stir mixture into sauce. Simmer until thickened.

Honey Sage Pork Tenderloin

¼ cup soy sauce

2 tablespoons red wine vinegar

½ cup water

¼ cup honey

2-3 tablespoons fresh sage

1 tablespoon minced garlic

1 tablespoon fresh ginger

1 teaspoon paprika

Salt and pepper to taste

2 (1 pound) pork tenderloins

Kosher salt to taste

Combine soy sauce and next 7 ingredients in small bowl, mixing well. Season with salt and pepper to taste. Place tenderloins in large zip-top plastic bag. Pour marinade into bag, seal and chill 4 to 6 hours. Preheat grill to medium heat. Spray grill rack with nonstick cooking spray. Remove tenderloins from bag, reserving marinade for sauce and lightly sprinkle with Kosher salt. Transfer to grill. Grill tenderloins over direct heat until meat thermometer inserted into thickest portion registers 150-160 degrees. Serve with Lemon Cilantro Sauce on the side. Yields 4-6 servings.

Lemon Cilantro Sauce:

Reserved marinade

½ cup butter

2 tablespoons lemon juice

2 tablespoons chopped cilantro

In small saucepan boil remaining marinade and reduce. Add butter, lemon juice and cilantro, stirring well.

Spicy Pork Tenderloin with Lime Mayonnaise

note...

Lime Mayonnaise may be prepared ahead, covered tightly and chilled up to 3 days.

1	tablespoon minced garlic	1/2	teaspoon black pepper
2	teaspoons paprika	2	(1 pound) pork tenderloins
1	teaspoon salt	2	(1 pound) loaves French bread,
1	teaspoon oregano		thinly sliced
1	teaspoon cumin		Lime wedges, for garnish
1/2	teaspoon cayenne pepper		Fresh cilantro, for garnish

Combine garlic and next 6 ingredients in small bowl, mixing well. Rub mixture over pork. Wrap with plastic wrap and refrigerate overnight. Allow tenderloins to come to room temperature 30 minutes before roasting. Preheat oven to 425 degrees. Unwrap pork, place in roasting pan and roast 20 to 25 minutes or until meat thermometer inserted in thickest portion of tenderloin registers 150-160 degrees. Cool to room temperature. Slice tenderloin very thinly and serve on French bread with Lime Mayonnaise. Garnish with lime wedges and cilantro. Yields about 40 appetizer or 6 entree servings.

Lime Mayonnaise:
1   cup mayonnaise
2   tablespoons fresh lime juice
1   teaspoon lime zest
Salt and pepper to taste

Combine mayonnaise, lime juice and zest in small bowl, mixing well. Add salt and pepper to taste.

Peppered Pork Tenderloin

1	teaspoon white pepper		1	teaspoon thyme
2	teaspoons black pepper		2½	teaspoons salt
1	teaspoon cayenne pepper		½	cup butter, melted and divided
1	teaspoon oregano		2	large (1½ pound) pork tenderloins
2	teaspoons garlic powder		2	cans (10¾ ounce) French onion soup

Combine all peppers and next 4 ingredients and set aside. Place tenderloins in glass baking dish. Pour half of butter on tenderloins, coating well, and sprinkle with pepper mixture. Allow to sit 2 hours at room temperature. Preheat oven to 400 degrees. Bake for 5-10 minutes on each side. Brush with remaining butter. Broil about 15 minutes, turning once. Pour soup over tenderloins. Decrease heat to 400 degrees and bake for 10 additional minutes. Meat temperature should read 150-160 degrees at thickest portion. Yields 6-8 servings.

Eastern North Carolina Pork Barbecue

1	cup apple cider vinegar
2	tablespoons sugar
½	teaspoon salt
½	teaspoon cayenne pepper or red pepper flakes
¼	teaspoon black pepper
1	(4-6 pound) pork shoulder, roast or Boston butt
½	cup water or chicken broth
1-2	onions, quartered

Combine vinegar and next 4 ingredients in small bowl. Place meat and vinegar sauce in a 6-quart crockpot. Add water or chicken broth and onions. Cover and cook 10-12 hours at low setting or 300 degrees. Pull meat from bone, discarding fat and skin. Shred or chop meat. Serve with cooking sauce. Yields 6-8 servings.

note...
Barbecue may be cooked 5 to 6 hours at 275 degrees or until meat falls from bone. Serve on sandwich buns with coleslaw.

Best Baby Back Ribs

2   sides very lean baby back pork ribs
1½ cups beef consommé
2   tablespoons soy sauce or more to taste
½   teaspoon garlic salt
2   rounded teaspoons ground ginger
1   cup dark brown sugar

Cut between each rib with a sharp knife and separate. Combine consommé and remaining ingredients in small bowl, mixing well. Place ribs in roaster, add marinade and chill overnight. Preheat oven to 400 degrees. Remove ribs from roaster, reserving marinade. Place wire rack in roaster and return ribs to same pan. Cover with foil, tightly crimping edges around pan; cook 1 hour. Remove foil; pour off and discard drippings. Remove rack and arrange ribs on bottom of roaster. Pour reserved marinade over ribs. Reduce heat to 300 degrees and cook 1 hour. Reduce heat to 275 degrees and continue cooking 1 hour, 30 minutes, turning and rotating ribs occasionally. Yields 4-6 servings.

Western Style Baby Back Ribs

2   racks baby back ribs
Western style barbeque seasoning
1   teaspoon garlic salt
1   onion, chopped
2   tablespoons brown sugar
2   tablespoons paprika
1   teaspoon dry mustard
1   teaspoon chili powder
3   tablespoons Worcestershire sauce
¼   cup vinegar
1   cup tomato juice
¼   cup ketchup
½   cup water
Hot sauce

Preheat oven to 450 degrees. Place wire racks on top of broiler pan. Sprinkle ribs with seasoning and garlic salt; transfer ribs to broiler racks. Cook 30 minutes. Combine onion and remaining ingredients in medium saucepan; simmer 15 to 20 minutes and set aside. Reduce heat to 350 degrees. Pour onion mixture on ribs, being sure to coat well. Pour 1 cup water in bottom of broiler pan. Seal tightly with foil and bake for 1 hour, 30 minutes. Yields 4-6 servings.

Grilled Apricot Lamb Chops

8   lamb chops, 1-inch thick
Salt and pepper to taste
2   cups apricot preserves
1/2   cup dry white wine
1/4   cup lemon juice
2   teaspoons teriyaki sauce
1/8   teaspoon cayenne pepper

Season lamb chops on both sides with salt and pepper and set aside. Combine preserves and remaining ingredients in saucepan over medium heat and reduce to 1½ cups. Preheat grill to high heat. Place lamb on grill, basting until done (140 degrees for medium-rare). Serve remaining warmed sauce with lamb. Yields 8 servings.

Charcoaled Leg of Lamb

4   tablespoons soy sauce
4   tablespoons olive oil
6   garlic cloves, minced
2   teaspoons dried thyme
2   teaspoons fresh rosemary
1/2   teaspoon ginger
1/4-1/2   cup white wine
1   (6 pound) leg of lamb, butterflied

Combine soy sauce and next 6 ingredients in small bowl, mixing well. Pour over lamb, coating thoroughly. Refrigerate until 1 hour before grilling. Bring to room temperature. Preheat grill to high heat. Grill lamb 5 minutes on each side. Thin remaining marinade with white wine and continue to baste lamb. Reduce heat to medium and grill additional 10 minutes on each side (140 degrees) for medium-rare or until desired doneness is achieved. Yields 6-8 servings.

Spinach Chicken Crêpes

note...
- *Purchased rotisserie chicken, skinned and boned is a time-saving substitute for chicken breasts.*

6-8 boneless chicken breasts
1   cup butter, divided
1   cup chopped onion
2   garlic cloves, minced
4   cups mushrooms, sliced
1   cup white wine, divided
4   packages (10 ounce) chopped frozen spinach, thawed and drained
1   cup toasted pine nuts
4   packages (8 ounce) cream cheese, softened

1   cup fresh grated Parmesan cheese
3/4 cup picante sauce
3   jars (6 ounce) marinated artichoke hearts, drained; reserving liquid
2   teaspoons salt
2   teaspoons nutmeg
1   teaspoon white pepper
1   teaspoon black pepper
2   teaspoons Italian seasoning
1½ cups heavy cream

In large saucepan cover chicken with water and boil 20 to 25 minutes. Cool, cut into bite size pieces and set aside. In large stockpot melt 2 tablespoons butter and sauté onion and garlic 5 minutes. Add mushrooms and ½ cup wine; sauté 10 minutes. Add remaining butter, spinach and nuts. Sauté 15 minutes, stirring often. Gradually add cream cheese, grated Parmesan cheese and picante sauce. Drain artichoke hearts, reserving ½ cup liquid. Add artichokes and reserved liquid. Add chicken, remaining ½ cup wine, salt and next 4 ingredients, stirring well. Remove from heat and whisk cream into mixture until smooth. Place 1 tablespoon chicken mixture in center of each crêpe. Roll and place in prepared shallow baking dish. Cover and bake at 350 degrees for 45 minutes. Top with sauce and serve. Yields 8-10 servings.

- *Frozen crêpes are available at most grocery stores.*

Crêpes:
1   cup all-purpose flour
2   eggs
½   cup milk
½   cup water
¼   teaspoon salt
2   tablespoons butter, melted

Place flour and remaining ingredients in blender. Blend until smooth. Batter should be consistency of heavy cream. Over low-medium heat, pour enough batter into 6-inch nonstick skillet to coat. Cook about 30 seconds to 1 minute. Crêpe is ready when sides lift easily away from skillet. Lift crêpe from skillet using spatula and place on waxed paper. If using crêpe maker, follow directions accordingly. Yields approximately 18-20 crêpes.

Italian Chicken

2	tablespoons olive oil	1	can (4 ounce) chopped black olives
1	tablespoon garlic salt	1	can (14 ounce) artichoke hearts
2	tablespoons balsamic vinegar	1	can (14½ ounce) Italian style tomatoes
½	cup chopped red onion	1	can (6 ounce) tomato paste
½	cup chopped celery	1	can (14 ounce) crushed tomatoes
1	tablespoon oregano	3	boneless, skinless chicken breasts
1	tablespoon Italian seasoning		Spaghetti
2	cans (4½ ounce)		Salt and pepper to taste
	sliced mushrooms		Romano cheese, shredded

Combine oil and next 6 ingredients in Dutch oven over medium heat. Sauté 3 to 4 minutes or until vegetables are tender. Add mushrooms and next 6 ingredients. Add enough water to cover chicken and cook 20 to 25 minutes on medium heat. Remove chicken and shred; return shredded chicken to Dutch oven. Add spaghetti to boiling sauce; cook 15 minutes or until al dente. Season with salt and pepper to taste. Serve in individual soup bowls topped with Romano cheese. Yields 6-8 servings.

Garlic Sour Cream Chicken

6	boneless, skinless chicken breasts, halved	2	teaspoons Worcestershire sauce
		1	teaspoon lemon juice
¾	cup sour cream		Salt and pepper to taste
4	garlic cloves, crushed	¾	cup breadcrumbs
1	teaspoon celery salt	½	cup butter, melted
½	teaspoon paprika		

Preheat oven to 350 degrees. Wash chicken well and pat dry. In medium bowl combine sour cream and next 5 ingredients, mixing well. Season with salt and pepper to taste. Dredge chicken breasts in mixture. In small bowl combine breadcrumbs and butter. Arrange chicken in prepared baking dish and top with breadcrumb mixture. Bake for 1 hour, 15 minutes or until brown. Yields 6 servings.

Chicken with Spicy Peanut Sauce

Marinade:

2¹/₂-3 pounds chicken pieces
6   tablespoons soy sauce
1   tablespoon honey
1   tablespoon coriander seed
2   garlic cloves, minced
2   teaspoons peeled, finely grated fresh ginger
¹/₄   teaspoon cayenne pepper

Cut chicken breasts in half; separate thighs and legs and set aside. In large bowl combine soy sauce and remaining ingredients, mixing well. Add chicken and coat thoroughly. Marinate 3 hours or overnight in refrigerator. Remove chicken from marinade. Broil or grill chicken about 30 minutes or until tender and browned, turning once. Serve with Spicy Peanut Sauce. Yields 4 servings.

Spicy Peanut Sauce:

4   tablespoons peanut butter
4   tablespoons soy sauce
2   tablespoons fresh lemon juice
¹/₄   cup firmly packed brown sugar
1   teaspoon cayenne pepper
¹/₄   cup cooking oil

Place peanut butter and remaining ingredients in food processor or blender. Process until smooth. In small saucepan heat sauce briefly before serving with chicken.

Chicken Dijonnaise

1/2	cup butter	2	garlic cloves, minced
4	(6 ounce) boneless, skinless chicken breasts	4	artichoke hearts, quartered
		4	tablespoons Dijon mustard
1/4	cup all-purpose flour	3/4	cup chicken broth or white wine
1	small yellow onion, thinly sliced	1/2	cup heavy cream
		1	tablespoon chopped parsley
1/2	cup sliced mushrooms		

Melt butter in large skillet over medium heat. Dredge chicken in flour; lightly brown in skillet on one side 2 to 3 minutes. Turn chicken and immediately add onions, mushrooms, garlic and artichoke hearts. Brown additional 2 to 3 minutes more. Add mustard and chicken broth; simmer uncovered until liquid is reduced by half (about 10 minutes). Add cream and cook 3 to 4 minutes until sauce is creamy. Remove chicken from skillet and drizzle with sauce. Sprinkle with parsley. Serve with pasta or rice pilaf. Yields 4 servings.

note...
- *Have all preparation work done before heating butter, so dish may be assembled quickly.*

Chicken in Roquefort Sauce

1/4	cup butter
1	chicken, cut up
1	pound sliced mushrooms
3	garlic cloves, minced
1	cup sour cream
4	ounces Roquefort cheese

Melt butter in skillet over medium heat. Brown chicken in butter. Transfer to casserole dish. Sauté mushrooms in skillet; add garlic, sour cream and cheese and simmer until thickened. Pour over chicken and bake at 350 degrees for 1 hour. Serve with pasta, mashed potatoes or rice. Yields 3-4 servings.

- *This dish may also be prepared using 3 whole breasts or 6 boneless, skinless chicken thighs.*

Curry Chicken with Tomatoes and Raisins

3   boneless, skinless
    chicken breasts
Salt to taste
Freshly ground black pepper to taste
3   tablespoons butter
1   onion, chopped
1   red bell pepper, julienned
½   cup dry white wine
3   garlic cloves, minced

1½ teaspoons curry powder
2   cans (14½ ounce) whole tomatoes,
    crushed and undrained or
    3½ cups fresh diced tomatoes
½   cup dried currants or ⅓ cup raisins
Cayenne pepper to taste
¼   cup toasted almond slivers
¼ -½ cup water, optional

Season chicken with salt and pepper. Melt butter in large skillet over medium-high heat. Brown chicken in skillet about 4 minutes on each side. Transfer chicken to platter. Reduce heat to medium and add onion, bell pepper and wine. Sauté until vegetables are just tender and skillet is deglazed. Add garlic and curry powder. Stir 1 minute. Add tomatoes and bring mixture to a simmer. Return chicken and juices that may have accumulated on platter to skillet. Cover and simmer about 10 minutes. Uncover and add currants or raisins. Add optional water or additional white wine if sauce is too thick. Cook until chicken is tender (about 5 minutes). Adjust seasonings with salt, pepper and cayenne pepper. Arrange chicken on serving platter. Spoon vegetables and sauce over chicken. Sprinkle with toasted almonds. Serve with steamed rice. Yields 4-6 servings.

Easy Hawaiian Chicken

8   chicken breasts
Salt and pepper to taste
1   bottle dark Russian dressing
1   package (1¼ ounce) dry onion soup mix
1   jar (10 ounce) peach preserves or orange marmalade

Season chicken breasts with salt and pepper. Combine dressing, soup mix and preserves, blending well. Pour half of dressing mixture into shallow glass casserole dish. Place chicken in single layer in casserole. Pour remaining dressing over chicken. Cover tightly and chill overnight. Bake, uncovered, at 325 degrees for 1 hour or until chicken is tender. Yields 8 servings.

Mediterranean Chicken

5-6 garlic cloves, minced
2 tablespoons dried oregano
¼ cup red wine vinegar
¼ cup olive oil
½ cup pitted prunes, diced
½ cup pitted green olives, sliced
⅓ cup capers, drained and rinsed

3 bay leaves
½ cup brown sugar
½ cup white wine
Salt to taste
Fresh ground pepper to taste
8-10 chicken breast halves
¼ cup finely chopped cilantro

Combine garlic and next 11 ingredients in small bowl, mixing well. Pour mixture over chicken. Cover tightly and chill overnight. Preheat oven to 350 degrees. Arrange chicken in single layer in shallow roasting pan. Spoon marinade over chicken. Bake for 50 minutes to 1 hour, basting frequently with pan juices. Transfer chicken to serving platter, sprinkle with cilantro and serve with remaining sauce. Yields 8-10 servings.

note...

- *If using boneless, skinless chicken breasts, cooking time may be reduced to 25 to 30 minutes.*

French Bistro Grilled Chicken

3 (3 pound) chickens
4 rosemary sprigs, leaves removed
10 dried bay leaves
10 garlic cloves, peeled
¼ cup dried thyme

¼ cup dried oregano
Juice of 3 lemons
2 tablespoons kosher salt
½ teaspoon black or white pepper
1½ cups olive oil

Split each chicken in half through the breastbone. Cut each half into leg-thigh quarters and breast-wing quarters; set aside. Place rosemary and next 7 ingredients in food processor and process until a paste forms. With processor running, pour in oil and process until a thick marinade forms. Place chicken and marinade in nonmetal dish; cover with plastic wrap. Chill 2 to 3 days, turning once. (It is best to marinate at least 2 days.) Preheat oven to 400 degrees. Roast, uncovered, 25 minutes. Remove chicken from roasting pan and finish cooking over charcoal grill, or broil in oven, about 5 to 7 minutes, turning several times. Yields 6-10 servings.

- *Whole chickens may be substituted with 9 pounds of chicken quarters.*

Creamy Poblano Chicken with Cornbread Waffles

3	tablespoons butter	1	teaspoon salt
1	large sweet onion, chopped	1/2	teaspoon pepper
2	roasted and seeded poblano chilies, chopped	1	can (10¾ ounce) cream of chicken with mushroom soup, undiluted
3	garlic cloves, minced	1	carton (8 ounce) sour cream
8	boneless, skinless chicken breast halves, cubed	1/2-1	cup shredded sharp Cheddar cheese
			Chopped chives, for garnish

Melt butter in Dutch oven over medium heat. Add onion, chili peppers and garlic and sauté 5 minutes. Add chicken, salt and pepper. Cook, stirring often, 8 to 10 minutes or until chicken is done. Stir in soup and sour cream until smooth. Add cheese and cook 7 to 8 minutes or until cheese melts. Serve over Cornbread Waffles and garnish with chopped chives. Yields 6-8 servings.

Cornbread Waffles:

1½	cups cornmeal	1	large egg
1/2	cup all-purpose flour	1½	cups milk
2½	teaspoons baking powder	1/4	cup butter, melted
2	tablespoons sugar	1½	cups frozen white shoepeg corn, thawed
3/4	teaspoon salt		

Preheat waffle iron. Combine cornmeal and next 4 ingredients in large bowl and set aside. Combine egg, milk, butter and corn, stirring well. Add to cornmeal mixture, stirring until dry ingredients are moist. Pour mixture into prepared waffle iron and cook until crisp. Yields 12 (4-inch) waffles.

Tequila Chicken with Citrus Salsa

Marinade:

1/4 cup tequila

1 tablespoon salt

1 tablespoon sugar

3 tablespoons cilantro leaves, chopped

4 garlic cloves, minced

1/2 cup fresh lime juice

1 jalapeño pepper, seeded and sliced

1 1/2 cups extra virgin olive oil

6 boneless, skinless chicken breasts

In food processor or blender, combine tequila and next 7 ingredients. Process until well blended. Place chicken in large glass or ceramic bowl. Pour marinade over chicken and chill 3 hours. Remove chicken from marinade. Grill 4 to 5 minutes on each side until browned, basting with marinade. Thinly slice cooked chicken. May be served hot or cold with Citrus Salsa. Yields 6 servings.

Citrus Salsa:

4 oranges, peeled and sectioned

2 pink grapefruits, peeled and sectioned

2 cups diced fresh pineapple

1 medium red onion, thinly sliced

1/2 red bell pepper, seeded and chopped

2 tablespoons cilantro leaves, chopped

1 tablespoon balsamic vinegar

1 tablespoon sugar

In large bowl combine all salsa ingredients, mixing well, and chill until ready to serve.

Glazed Cornish Hens with Savory Stuffing

6   **Cornish game hens**
1/2   **cup lemon-lime soda**
1/2   **cup honey**
Salt to taste
2   **cups wild rice, cooked**
3/4   **pound hot pork sausage**

Cook rice according to package directions. Crumble and sauté sausage until cooked. Add to rice and mix well; set aside. Combine soda and honey. With a pastry brush, baste hens thoroughly. Continue to baste refrigerated hens every hour for 3 hours. Lightly season hen cavities with salt, stuff with dressing. Bake at 325 degrees for 1 hour. Increase heat to 350 degrees and bake 30 additional minutes or until tender. Yields 6 servings.

Game Day Turkey Tailgate Sandwich

note...
- *May substitute jarred roasted red peppers from grocery store.*

- *Make additional sandwiches for a crowd. Feel free to use your favorite deli meats.*

1   **large red bell pepper**
1   **thin and crusty French bread loaf**
1   **tablespoon extra virgin olive oil**
1   **tablespoon red wine vinegar**

2-3 **thin mozzarella cheese slices**
4-6 **arugula or radicchio leaves**
4   **thin tomato slices**
Freshly ground black pepper to taste
4   **thin smoked ham slices**
4   **thin smoked turkey or chicken slices**

Preheat broiler. Cut pepper in half lengthwise and remove core, seeds and ribs. Flatten slightly and place on aluminum foil, skin side up. Place under broiler until skin is charred black. Transfer to plastic zip-top bag, seal and let steam 10 minutes. Peel and discard skin; set roasted pepper halves aside. Trim off ends of bread until 12-inch length remains. Cut in half lengthwise and scoop out center. Brush cut sides with olive oil and vinegar. Arrange mozzarella slices on bottom half; layer arugula and tomato slices, covering length of bread. Season with pepper. Cut each roasted pepper half lengthwise; place over tomatoes. Top with ham and turkey or chicken slices and replace with top half of bread. Press sandwich to flatten slightly and wrap tightly in plastic wrap. Let sit at room temperature at least 1 hour. Before serving, unwrap sandwich and cut in half crosswise. Yields 2 servings.

Game

Café

Notes...

● *Duck meat is rich and flavorful. Choose a fresh duck with a broad, plump breast with elastic, not saggy, skin. Make sure the packaging is tight and unbroken if purchasing frozen duck.*

Game

Spicy Dove Bites. 98

Carolina Barbecue Doves. 98

Indian-Spiced Squab 99

Chili Rubbed Quail 99

Savory Northern Italian Quail
with Polenta 100

Braised Quail with Grapes. 101

Raspberry Glazed Quail 101

Grilled Quail. 102

Rosemary Fried Quail 102

Roast Quail with Hazelnuts and Port 103

Bourbon Molasses Quail
or Duck Breasts 104

Hunter's Duck Ragu with Pappardelle 105

Crocked Ducks 105

Peking Spiced Duck 106

Peppered Duck Breasts 106

Rabbit Cacciatore 107

Grilled Venison Tenderloin with
Red Currant Glaze 108

Texas Venison Chili 109

Knock Your Socks Off
Wild Game Marinade 110

Venison Backstrap with
Savory Sage Marinade 110

Spicy Dove Bites

note...

Fat-free Italian dressing is not recommended.

12 dove breasts
1   onion, cut in strips (½-inch x 1-inch)
12 pickled jalapeño peppers, cut in strips (½-inch x 1-inch)
1   green bell pepper, cut in strips (½-inch x 1-inch)
1   bottle (8 ounce) Italian dressing
12 lean bacon slices, cut in half

Slide sharp knife along each side of breast bone to remove breasts (about the size of a half-dollar). Place breast halves in small bowl, then place vegetables in small separate bowls. Divide dressing between bowls to marinate. Cover and chill overnight. Place 1 breast fillet near end of bacon slice. Place onion strip, jalapeño strip and bell pepper strip next to breast. Fold bacon over and roll into small roll; secure with toothpick. Repeat process with remaining breast fillets. Bake at 350 degrees for 20 minutes or until bacon is done or preferably grill, turning frequently until bacon is done. Yields 24 appetizer servings.

Carolina Barbecue Doves

24 doves
Butter, for browning
1½ cups vinegar
1   teaspoon cayenne pepper
    or to taste
½   teaspoon black pepper

2   tablespoons chili powder
1   teaspoon dry mustard
2   teaspoons Worcestershire sauce
Salt to taste
Dash of hot sauce

In large skillet brown doves in melted butter. Combine vinegar and remaining ingredients in large bowl. Add doves, tossing to coat. Transfer to casserole dish and bake at 350 degrees for 2 hours. Serve Carolina style with corn on the cob, cole slaw, barbecued beans and slices of white sandwich bread. Yields 8-12 servings.

Indian-Spiced Squab

1	teaspoon salt	3	tablespoons plain low-fat yogurt
1	teaspoon cumin	4	squab or other game hen,
1	teaspoon dry mustard		washed and patted dry
1	teaspoon turmeric	1	large onion, cut into 8 pieces
1	teaspoon paprika	1	lime, halved and cut across
1/2	teaspoon ground cardamom		into 1/4-inch-thick slices
1/2	teaspoon cinnamon	16	fresh cilantro sprigs
1/4	teaspoon cayenne pepper		

Preheat oven to 425 degrees. Combine salt and next 8 ingredients in small bowl, mixing well. Stuff each squab cavity with 1 piece onion, 2 pieces lime and 4 cilantro sprigs. Rub skin with yogurt-spice mixture. Marinate at room temperature for 1 hour. Place squab in roasting pan and tie legs together with cooking string to close the cavities. Roast until juices run slightly pink when pricked with fork in thickest portion of leg (about 25 to 30 minutes). Let stand 10 minutes. Remove string and transfer to 4 individual serving plates. Serve with rice and vegetable of choice. Yields 4 servings.

Chili Rubbed Quail

6	quail
1	tablespoon chili powder
2	teaspoons dill seeds
1	teaspoon lemon pepper
1/2	teaspoon cumin
1/4	cup butter, softened

Combine chili powder and remaining ingredients; rub quail with mixture. Roast at 375 degrees for about 20 minutes or until tender and brown or grill for about 10 minutes away from coals, turning once. Yields 4-6 servings.

note...

- *This recipe is also delicious with cornish game hens, whole chicken or with pork tenderloin.*

- *For a delicious alternative to white rice, see the following recipes:* Herbed Wild Rice with Toasted Pine Nuts *or* Herbed Couscous with Feta *(page 152).*

- *Chili Rub is also delicious on salmon steaks.*

Savory Northern Italian Quail with Polenta

Quails:

12 fresh rosemary sprigs
8   quails, wing tips removed
Salt to taste
Freshly ground black pepper to taste
16 thin pancetta slices or lean bacon

Preheat oven to 425 degrees. Place 1 rosemary sprig in each quail cavity. Lightly salt and pepper birds. Wrap 2 pieces of pancetta or bacon around each quail and tie with string. Set aside. Prepare polenta. Roast quail in oven 10-12 minutes, then remove string. Top each serving of polenta with 2 quail. Garnish with remaining rosemary sprig and serve immediately. Yields 4 servings.

Polenta:

2½ cups water
2   teaspoons salt
½ cup yellow cornmeal
¾ cup grated Parmesan cheese
Freshly ground black pepper

Combine water and salt in medium saucepan. Bring to a boil over medium heat. Whisking constantly, add cornmeal gradually, pouring in light, steady stream. Reduce heat to a slow simmer, stirring constantly with wooden spoon until thickened (about 10 minutes). Add pepper and grated Parmesan, stirring well. Divide polenta among 4 plates and place in a 150-degree oven to keep warm.

Braised Quail with Grapes

6   quail, halved
Salt and pepper to taste
1/4   cup all-purpose flour
4   tablespoons butter
1   tablespoon olive oil

1-2   shallots, minced
1   cup chicken broth, divided
1   tablespoon lemon juice
1   cup seedless grapes, red or white

Wash quail and pat dry. Combine salt, pepper and flour. Dredge birds in seasoned flour, shaking off excess flour. In skillet heat butter and oil until hot. Cook birds until brown on all sides. Add 1/2 cup broth. Simmer until quail is thoroughly cooked. Transfer to a plate and keep warm. Add shallots to skillet; saute until tender. Add remaining 1/2 cup broth, lemon juice and grapes. Reduce liquids by half. Add quails to warm through. Serve with wild rice. Yields 4-6 servings.

Raspberry Glazed Quail

6   quail, boned and opened flat (leg and wing remain intact)
1   egg, beaten
10   crackers, crushed or 1 cup Panko (Japanese) bread crumbs
Salt and pepper to taste
3-4   tablespoons butter
1/4-1/2 cup raspberry syrup
1   cup fresh raspberries

Preheat oven to 350 degrees. Wash quail and pat dry. Dredge in egg, then crackers or Panko crumbs. Lightly salt and pepper. Heat butter in skillet. Quickly brown quail on each side. Transfer to baking sheet with raised edges; drizzle with raspberry syrup. Place in oven to finish cooking and to glaze (about 5-7 minutes). Raspberries may be placed around birds in oven or simply used to garnish plates. Yields 4-6 servings.

note...

- *Wild game quail may be smaller than farm-raised birds.*

- *Herbed Wild Rice with Toasted Pine Nuts (page 152) is an excellent accompaniment.*

- *Your butcher can debone the cavity of the quail. The leg and wing bones will remain intact.*

note...

● *Side suggestions:*
Herbed Wild Rice
with Toasted Pine
Nuts, Herbed
Couscous with Feta
(page 152),
Decadent but
Delicious Cheese
Grits (page 155),
Gruyère Potato
Gratin (page 157) or
Savory Sweet Potato
Gratin (page 159).

Grilled Quail

16	whole quail breasts	16	thin bacon slices
3	jalapeño peppers, sliced crosswise ¼-inch thick	3	tablespoons molasses
1	medium onion, halved and sliced ¼ inch thick	2	tablespoons olive oil
		2	teaspoons sherry
		⅓	cup cornmeal

Salt and pepper to taste

Preheat charcoal grill. Arrange quail breasts skin side down on large platter. Place one jalapeño slice and several onion rings in center of each breast. Season with salt and pepper and fold breasts together to enclose the filling. Wrap bacon slice around each breast and secure with wooden toothpick. In small bowl combine molasses, oil and sherry. Brush stuffed quail with glaze and sprinkle with cornmeal. Season with salt and pepper. Grill quail breasts over medium-hot fire, turning until crisp and medium rare (about 9 minutes). Serve hot with wild rice. Yields 16 servings.

note...

● *The quail will not*
absorb too much oil
if maintained at
325 degrees.

Rosemary Fried Quail

8	whole quail (with or without breastbone)	1	teaspoon salt
1	cup buttermilk	½	teaspoon pepper
1	cup all-purpose flour	2-3	cups cooking oil
1	cup rice flour or cornstarch	4-6	fresh rosemary sprigs

Wash quail and pat dry. Soak in buttermilk and chill 1 to 2 hours. Combine flour and rice flour or cornstarch; season with salt and pepper. Heat oil in deep skillet to 350 degrees. Remove chicken from buttermilk and coat with seasoned flour mixture. Place quail in hot oil. (Oil should bubble vigorously.) Cook on first side about 5 minutes, lifting to see if browning evenly. Adjust heat if browning too quickly. After 5 to 10 minutes, turn over. Cook about 5 minutes. Add rosemary sprigs to frying pan and continue to fry about 1 minute more. Transfer to wire rack set over paper towels. Quail will drain and remain crisp. Yields 8 servings.

Roast Quail with Hazelnuts and Port

6   tablespoons cold unsalted butter, divided
1/2 cup thinly sliced shallots
2   cups ruby port
2   cups chicken stock
1   cup toasted hazelnuts, divided
2   tablespoons clarified unsalted butter, divided (see below)
6   partially boned quail, trussed
Salt and pepper to taste

Sauce: Make sauce ahead of serving. Refrigerate and reheat before serving. In medium, non-metallic saucepan, melt 1 tablespoon butter. Add shallots and cook over moderately low heat, until softened but not browned (about 2 minutes). Add port and boil over moderately high heat until reduced to $3/4$ cup (about 15 minutes). Add stock and boil until reduced to $1^1/8$ cups (about 15 minutes). Strain sauce into small, non-reactive saucepan. Set aside.

Quail: In food processor grind half of hazelnuts to a paste and transfer mixture to small bowl. Finely chop remaining nuts and stir into hazelnut paste along with 1 tablespoon clarified butter and set aside. Preheat oven to 475 degrees. Remove breast bones from quail, being sure to leave legs and wings intact. In large, heavy skillet, warm $1/2$ tablespoon clarified butter. Add 3 quail, breast side down, and season with salt and pepper. Cook over high heat until browned (about 2 minutes). Transfer quail, breast side up, to prepared baking sheet and season with salt and pepper. Wipe out skillet and repeat with remaining $1/2$ tablespoon clarified butter and 3 quail. Let cool. Pat hazelnut mixture onto quail and roast in center of oven 4 to 5 minutes for medium rare. Let rest 10 minutes before serving. Yields 6 quail.

Meanwhile, reheat sauce over moderate heat. Cut remaining 5 tablespoons of cold butter into $1/2$-inch pats. Briskly whisk in butter over low heat, 1 piece at a time, until smooth. Season with salt and pepper. Remove sauce from heat, but keep warm. Serve quail topped with 2 tablespoons of sauce around each bird. Pass remaining sauce separately.

Clarified butter:
6   tablespoons cold unsalted butter

Melt butter in a heavy saucepan over low heat. Remove pan from heat and set aside 5 minutes. Using a large spoon, carefully remove white foam from top of melted butter. Pour clear liquid into an airtight container. Keep refrigerated. Makes $1/3$ cup.

note...

To toast hazelnuts, preheat oven to 350 degrees. Spread hazelnuts on pie plate and toast about 10 minutes. Wrap in kitchen towel and rub gently to remove skins. Cool before using.

note...

*Let duck sit
5 minutes; slice to
desired thickness.*

Bourbon Molasses Quail or Duck Breasts

Quail or Duck Breasts:

8	quail, breast bone removed or 2 duck breasts, skinned, bone removed	2	tablespoons bourbon
		2	tablespoons molasses
		2	tablespoons thyme leaves
1/2	teaspoon kosher salt	3	tablespoons olive oil
	Freshly ground black pepper to taste	8	thyme sprigs

Make Bourbon Molasses sauce and set aside. Reheat before serving. Wash and pat birds dry. Season all sides lightly with salt and pepper; transfer to baking dish. In small bowl combine bourbon, molasses and thyme leaves. Spoon mixture over birds. Close quail cavity and tie legs together with cooking string. Heat oil in heavy skillet until hot. Place quail breast side down or duck breast laid flat in oil. Place a second heavy skillet on top of birds or duck breasts and reduce heat, cooking 3 minutes. Remove top skillet, turn birds or duck breasts and cook 3 to 4 additional minutes or until birds are done. Duck breasts will be medium-rare. Spoon Bourbon Molasses sauce over birds and garnish with thyme sprigs. Serve with wild rice. Yields 8 servings.

Sauce:

1	tablespoon peanut oil	1/4	cup molasses
16	reserved quail wing tips or 2 tablespoons duck fat, skin attached	1/4	cup cider vinegar
		6	cups chicken broth
		2	thyme sprigs
3	shallots, sliced	1/2	teaspoon kosher salt
4	garlic cloves, minced	1/2	teaspoon freshly ground black pepper
1/2	cup bourbon		

Heat oil and add wing tips or duck fat in large heavy saucepan. Cook 3 to 4 minutes until crispy. Add shallots and garlic and cook about 1 minute until tender. Add bourbon, molasses, vinegar and chicken broth. Bring to a boil, then reduce to a simmer until reduced to $1^1/2$ cups. (This will take about 30 to 45 minutes.) Add thyme sprigs during last 15 minutes. Remove thyme sprigs, add salt and pepper. Sauce may be reheated in order to serve with warm quail or duck breasts.

Hunter's Duck Ragu with Pappardelle

4	ducks, skin removed	1-2	celery stalks, diced
1	ounce dried porcini mushrooms	1	cup red wine
2-4	tablespoons olive oil	1	can (28 ounce)
1/4	cup chopped pancetta or		whole roma tomatoes
	6 chopped bacon slices, blanched	1	cup chicken broth
1	sweet onion, chopped	1	teaspoon salt
2	carrots, peeled and		Pepper to taste
	finely chopped	1	pound pappardelle pasta
3-4	garlic cloves, sliced		(or other wide pasta)

note...
To remove some of
the smoky flavor
of bacon, cook, or
blanch, in boiling
water for 3 minutes.
Drain.

Wash ducks and pat dry. Discard all but legs, thighs and breasts. Soak mushrooms 15 to 20 minutes in 1/2 cup warm water and drain, reserving mushroom broth. In large heavy stockpot heat olive oil until hot. Add pancetta and render some fat. Add duck pieces and brown on all sides. Remove duck and set aside. Add onion, carrot, garlic, celery and mushrooms. Cook until tender (about 5 to 7 minutes). Add wine, tomatoes, chicken broth and mushroom broth. Be careful to omit any sand from mushroom broth. Bring to a boil and add duck pieces. Cover and simmer 1 hour. Remove duck, cool and debone. Return meat to stockpot and simmer 30 minutes. Add salt and pepper to taste. Boil pasta according to package directions in salted water and drain. Add pasta to sauce, tossing to coat, and cook 1 minute. Yields 6-8 servings.

Crocked Ducks

2	mallard or other game ducks	1/2	teaspoon onion powder
1/2	teaspoon chicken bouillon	1/2	cup sherry
	granules	1	teaspoon cornstarch dissolved
1/2	cup water		in 3 tablespoons water
1/2	teaspoon garlic powder		

Rub ducks generously inside and out with salt. Place in crockpot. Dissolve bouillon in water; add garlic powder and onion powder. Combine with sherry and pour over ducks. Cook on low 8 to 10 hours or until meat falls off bone easily. Thicken drippings with cornstarch mixture for gravy if desired. Yields 6 servings.

Peking Spiced Duck

4-6	dried mushrooms	1	duck (4-5 pound)
2	cups water	1	chicken bouillon cube
3	medium onions, chopped	4½	cups water or chicken broth
5	tablespoons cooking oil, divided	1½	cups red wine
		1½	teaspoons soy sauce
4	tablespoons fresh ginger, peeled and chopped	1	teaspoon black pepper
		3-4	leeks, cut into 2-inch strips

Preheat oven to 350 degrees. Soak mushrooms in 2 cups water 30 minutes. In skillet sauté onions and leeks in 4 tablespoons oil 5 minutes. Transfer to bowl and set aside. Add fresh ginger to skillet. Brown duck in remaining 1 tablespoon oil on all sides 6 to 10 minutes. Drain and slice mushrooms. Add to onions and leeks. Stuff duck with onion mixture. Transfer to baking dish. Combine bouillon and next 4 ingredients in large bowl. Spoon half of wine mixture over duck. Cover and bake for 1 hour, 30 minutes, to 2 hours or until tender. Baste occasionally. When duck is finished, remove stuffing from cavity and add to pan juices to make a sauce. Cut meat from bone; slice breasts and legs in half. Serve with warm sauce and wild rice. Yields 6-8 servings.

Peppered Duck Breasts

Wild duck breasts, breast bone removed
Buttermilk or whole milk
All-purpose flour
Freshly ground coarse black pepper
½ cup butter
½ cup red wine

Soak wild duck breasts in buttermilk 6 to 8 minutes. Remove breasts from milk and coat in flour. Season heavily with coarse pepper. Melt butter in skillet and cook 3 to 5 minutes on each side. Transfer breasts to a plate and keep warm. Deglaze skillet with wine and boil to reduce slightly. Add breasts to sauce and heat through. One whole wild duck breast yields 4 servings.

Rabbit Cacciatore

$1/2$	cup all-purpose flour
1	teaspoon salt
1	teaspoon pepper
1	rabbit, cut into serving pieces
4	tablespoons olive oil
1	sweet onion, chopped
2	jalapeño peppers, seeded and chopped
$1/2$	pound mixed wild or button mushrooms

$1/4$-$1/3$	cup sun-dried tomatoes, cut into strips
1-2	tablespoons sugar
2	cups white wine
	Juice and zest of 1 orange
1	cup chunky tomato sauce or pasta sauce
2	tablespoons fresh rosemary, chopped

Combine flour, salt and pepper. Rinse rabbit, pat dry and dredge in flour. In heavy skillet heat oil until hot. In batches cook rabbit until brown. Transfer rabbit to plate and set aside. Add onion and next 4 ingredients to skillet. Cook until onions are tender (about 10 minutes). Add wine, juice of orange and tomato sauce; bring to a boil. Add rabbit; simmer on low heat 45 minutes or until meat is tender and sauce thickens. Add rosemary and zest. Serve over polenta or wide noodles. Yields 4-6 servings.

note...

- *Rabbit is readily available if ordered ahead at most grocery butcher counters.*

- *Side suggestions:* Fast and Easy Polenta with Roasted Vegetables *(page 154) or* Decadent but Delicious Cheese Grits *(page 155).*

Grilled Venison Tenderloin with Red Currant Glaze

note...

Marinade may be frozen indefinitely or refrigerated for up to one week.

Venison:

1½ cups cooking oil		1 tablespoon black pepper	
¾ cup soy sauce		½ cup red wine vinegar	
¼ cup Worcestershire sauce		1½ teaspoons dried parsley flakes	
2 tablespoons dry mustard		2-3 garlic cloves, minced	
2 teaspoons salt		1 venison tenderloin	
½ cup lemon juice			

Combine oil and next 9 ingredients in medium bowl and mix well. Pour marinade into plastic freezer bag with tenderloin; chill 6 to 8 hours. Grill tenderloin 20 minutes or until medium rare, turning occasionally, or bake in oven at 400 degrees for 15-20 minutes. Serve with Red Currant Glaze. Yields 6-8 servings.

Red Currant Glaze:

½ cup dried currants

2 tablespoons dry sherry

1 jar (10 ounce) currant jelly

1 tablespoon soy sauce

Plump currants in sherry 15 minutes. Combine currants with sherry, jelly and soy sauce. Heat over low heat until jelly melts, stirring constantly. Water may be added for a thinner sauce.

Texas Venison Chili

2	red onions, chopped	$^1/_3$	cup chili powder
6	garlic cloves, minced	2-3	bay leaves
2	tablespoons cooking oil	4	whole cloves
2	pounds ground venison	2	cinnamon sticks
1	yellow bell pepper, seeded and chopped	2	teaspoons cumin
		2	teaspoons salt
1	red bell pepper, seeded and chopped	2	teaspoons black pepper
		1-1$^1/_2$	teaspoons cayenne pepper
8-10	jalapeño peppers, seeded and chopped	1-1$^1/_2$	teaspoons celery salt
		1-1$^1/_2$	teaspoons oregano
3	cans (14$^1/_2$ ounce) whole tomatoes, chopped	1-1$^1/_2$	teaspoons sage
		1-1$^1/_2$	teaspoons paprika
1-2	cans (15 ounce) pinto beans, drained and rinsed	2	cans (12 ounce) beer
			Cheddar cheese, for garnish
$^1/_2$	cup parsley, chopped		Sour cream, for garnish

In Dutch oven sauté onions and garlic in oil. Remove and set aside. Brown venison in Dutch oven. Add onions, garlic, chopped peppers, tomatoes, beans and parsley, mixing well. Add chili powder and next 11 ingredients, mixing well. Add beer; simmer 1 hour, adding water as needed for desired consistency. Remove cinnamon sticks before serving. Garnish individual servings with cheese or a dollop of sour cream. Serve over corn chips, if desired. Yields 8-10 servings.

Knock Your Socks Off Wild Game Marinade

½ cup butter	½ tablespoon salt
⅔ cup white vinegar	½ tablespoon pepper
1 teaspoon garlic powder	1 tablespoon Worcestershire sauce
1 teaspoon dry mustard	½ teaspoon cayenne pepper
1 teaspoon hot sauce	

Melt butter in small saucepan; add remaining ingredients. Bring to just a boil and remove from heat. Cool 45 minutes. Pour over any game steaks, venison, boar or pork chops. Chill in marinade 2 hours or overnight. Grill meat and discard marinade. It is NOT a sauce.

Venison Backstrap with Savory Sage Marinade

1-2 venison backstraps (tenderloins)

Prepare marinade and pour over backstrap to cover. Refrigerate overnight. Bring backstrap to room temperature before grilling. Remove excess marinade to prevent flaming during grilling. Lightly sprinkle with additional kosher salt. Grill backstrap on preheated grill, 8 minutes per side or until medium-rare. Do not overcook. Let rest 5-10 minutes before slicing. Yields 6-8 servings.

Savory Sage Marinade:
1-2 teaspoons kosher salt
Freshly ground black pepper to taste
3 shallots
10 garlic cloves, peeled
1 package fresh sage, stems removed, washed and dried
1 cup olive oil
Additional kosher salt and freshly ground pepper to taste

Place salt and next 4 ingredients in food processor and process until garlic is minced, gradually adding olive oil.

Seafood

Tower Bridge
by John Cook

sponsored by

Notes...

- *Any firm fleshed white fish may be used in place of the fish recipes in this section (i.e. Chilean sea bass, sole, halibut, swordfish, orange roughy).*
- *A large, heavy pot with a tight fitting lid may be used in place of a Dutch oven.*
- *2-2½ pounds of shrimp in the shell yields one pound cooked, peeled shrimp, or 2 cups.*
- *To butterfly shrimp before cooking, peel the shrimp to the tail, leaving the tail intact. Devein the shrimp. Holding so the underside faces up, slice down its length almost to the vein. Spread and flatten.*

Seafood

Crabmeat Remick 112

Pasta Nests with Lump Crabmeat 112

New England Crab Cakes 113

The Best Crawfish Étouffée 113

Crawfish Tortellini 114

Shellfish Skewers with
Asian Dipping Sauce 114

Louisiana Seafood Gumbo 115

Shrimp and Sausage Jambalaya 116

Barbecue Shrimp 116

New Orleans Barbecued Shrimp 117

Shrimp and Jalapeño Brochettes 118

Spicy Cajun Shrimp 118

Favorite Mustard Marinated Shrimp 119

Shrimp Marsala 119

Paw Paw's Oysters Rockefeller 120

Thanksgiving Oysters 120

Glazed Grilled Salmon Fillet 121

Sautéed Salmon with Spinach 121

Grilled Salmon and Vegetable Salad 122

Easy But Elegant Salmon
en Papillote 123

Grilled Ponzu Marinated Salmon 123

Pine Nut Crusted Snapper 124

Crabmeat Remick

note...

- Remick sauce will separate if left in oven too long.

1/2 teaspoon dry mustard	1/2 cup chili sauce
1/2 teaspoon paprika	1 teaspoon tarragon vinegar
1/4 teaspoon celery salt	1/2 cup mayonnaise
1/4 teaspoon salt	1 pound lump crabmeat
Hot sauce to taste	6 slices cooked bacon

In medium bowl, combine mustard, paprika, salts and a few dashes of hot sauce. Add chili sauce and vinegar, mixing well. Blend in mayonnaise and set aside. Divide crabmeat among 6 ramekins placed on baking sheet. Broil until thoroughly hot. Remove from broiler and place bacon over hot crabmeat in each ramekin. Top with remick sauce. Heat ramekins under broiler a few seconds and serve immediately. Yields 6 servings.

Pasta Nests with Lump Crabmeat

- Pasta nests may be prepared several hours in advance and stored in plastic airtight bags.

- A "bird's nest basket" may be purchased at specialty cooking stores for ease in preparing pasta nests.

Cooking oil, for frying	1 cup heavy cream
1 package vermicelli or capellini pasta nests	Lemon pepper to taste
1/2 cup finely chopped onion	1/2 teaspoon cayenne pepper
2 tablespoons butter	Salt to taste
1/4 cup dry white wine	1 pound fresh lump crabmeat, rinsed and picked
1 tablespoon Dijon mustard	1 tablespoon capers, rinsed and drained
	Sun-dried tomatoes, for garnish

Cook pasta according to package directions until al dente. In medium saucepan pour 2 to 3 inches of oil for frying pasta. When oil is hot, place 3/4 cup pasta in metal strainer. Top with a second strainer of a smaller size or use a wooden spoon to press the pasta into the oil. Place in oil 1 to 2 minutes to crisp. Remove and drain on paper towels. In large skillet sauté onion in butter. Add wine and reduce until slightly thickened. Stir in mustard and cream, bringing to a boil. Add lemon pepper, cayenne and salt. Gently rinse crabmeat in a colander, checking for pieces of shell. Gently fold in crabmeat and capers. Taste for seasoning. Place a nest on a plate and top with crabmeat. Top with sun-dried tomatoes. Yields 6-8 servings.

New England Crab Cakes

¼ cup finely chopped onion	1 teaspoon lemon juice
¼ cup finely chopped celery	2 tablespoons chopped cilantro
4 tablespoons butter, melted	3 tablespoons pimento, chopped
2 eggs, beaten	Hot sauce to taste
1 pound lump crabmeat, rinsed and picked	Salt and pepper to taste
	Cooking oil, for frying
3 slices white bread, crusts removed and finely torn	Lemon wedges
	Sprigs of cilantro, for garnish
¼ cup mayonnaise	

Sauté onion and celery in butter about 4 minutes. Combine with remaining ingredients, mixing gently, and shape into cakes. Chill about 2 hours. Pour enough cooking oil into skillet to generously coat bottom. Heat oil until hot but not smoking. Cook cakes about 2 minutes on each side or until lightly browned. Serve with lemon wedges and sprigs of cilantro. Yields 6-8 servings.

The Best Crawfish Étouffée

1½ cups onion, chopped

½ cup butter

2 pounds crawfish meat, fresh or frozen

2 celery stalks, chopped

½ teaspoon cayenne pepper

1½ teaspoons salt

1 tablespoon flour

Cooked white rice

In Dutch oven sauté onions in butter. Add crawfish, stirring well. Add celery, cayenne, salt and flour, stirring well. Cover and allow liquid to thicken, stirring occasionally. Add water as needed. Serve with rice. Yields 6 servings.

note...
This recipe doubles well.

Crawfish Tortellini

1	medium onion, finely chopped	2	tablespoons parsley
2	garlic cloves, minced	1½	pints heavy cream
½	cup butter	1	tablespoon cornstarch
1-2	pounds crawfish tails, rinsed lightly	1	package (7 ounce) Parmesan cheese tortellini, cooked
½	cup Parmesan cheese		Ground red pepper to taste

In large saucepan sauté onion and garlic in butter. Add crawfish tails, cooking about 5 minutes. Add Parmesan cheese, parsley and heavy cream. Stir cornstarch in a little water; add to sauce to thicken. Boil tortellini according to package directions. Fold in tortellini; season with red pepper. Serve immediately or transfer to casserole dish and bake at 350 degrees until bubbling. Yields 6-8 servings.

Shellfish Skewers with Asian Dipping Sauce

note...
Asian Dipping Sauce *may be prepared up to four hours in advance.*

2	tablespoons peanut oil	2	teaspoons cornstarch
2	jalapeños, seeded and minced	1	tablespoon fresh lime juice
2	teaspoons minced peeled fresh ginger	¼	cup chopped fresh cilantro
1	garlic clove, minced	24	large uncooked shrimp, peeled and deveined
¾	cup dry white wine	24	large sea scallops
⅓	cup soy sauce	6	metal skewers
⅓	cup packed dark brown sugar		

Heat oil in small saucepan over low heat until warm. Stir in jalapeños, ginger and garlic. Cover and cook 6 minutes, stirring occasionally, being careful not to brown. Combine wine, soy sauce, sugar and cornstarch until dissolved. Add to jalapeño mixture; increase heat to medium-high and whisk until mixture comes to a boil and thickens slightly. Remove sauce from heat. Transfer to bowl and let cool to room temperature. Stir in lime juice and cilantro, mixing well. Pour ½ cup sauce into small bowl. Reserve remaining sauce for dipping. Prepare grill. Thread 4 shrimp and 4 scallops alternately onto 6 metal skewers. Place skewers on grill and brush with sauce. Turn over once and brush again with sauce. Grill until shrimp are pink. Serve shrimp and scallops with reserved Asian Dipping Sauce. Yields 6 servings.

Favorite Mustard Marinated Shrimp

1/4 cup tarragon vinegar
1/4 cup red wine vinegar
1 teaspoon pepper
1/4 cup dry mustard
1 teaspoon hot red pepper flakes
2 teaspoons salt
1/4 cup cooking oil
1/4 cup extra virgin olive oil
1/4 cup finely chopped
    fresh flat-leaf parsley

2 garlic cloves, minced
6 green onions, chopped
1/4 cup capers, rinsed and drained
1 lemon
1 garlic clove, flattened
1 package (3 ounce) shrimp boil
2 1/2 pounds medium shrimp,
    uncooked and peeled
Crackers
Cucumber slices

In large bowl whisk together vinegars, pepper, mustard, red pepper flakes and salt. Slowly pour in oils, continuing to whisk until mixture thickens slightly. Stir in parsley, garlic, green onions and capers; set aside. Boil lemon, flattened garlic and shrimp boil in 3 quarts water 5 minutes. Add shrimp to boiling water and cook, uncovered, just until pink (about 2 to 3 minutes). Drain shrimp and combine with marinade. Cover and chill overnight or up to 2 days. Drain marinade from shrimp and serve with crackers and chilled cucumber slices. Yields 8 to 10 servings.

Shrimp Marsala

1 pound sliced mushrooms
3 tablespoons butter
1 tablespoon flour
3 ounces dry Marsala wine
2 cups heavy cream
1/4 teaspoon lemon zest

1 1/2 teaspoons onion juice
1 rounded teaspoon chopped parsley
2 pounds shrimp, cooked and peeled
Breadcrumbs to cover
Parmesan cheese to cover

In large sauté pan, sauté mushrooms in butter. When tender, blend in flour. Add wine and stir. Add heavy cream, stirring until smooth and thick; add zest, onion juice, parsley and shrimp. Pour into casserole dish. Sprinkle with breadcrumbs and Parmesan cheese. Bake at 375 degrees for 15 minutes or until bubbling. Serve over rice or puff pastry. Yields 6 servings.

Paw Paw's Oysters Rockefeller

1½ tablespoons butter
1   tablespoon minced
    celery leaves
1   tablespoon dried parsley
1   medium yellow onion,
    finely chopped
½   teaspoon garlic powder
1   package (10 ounce)
    frozen spinach

1   tablespoon Worcestershire sauce
Juice of 1 lemon
½   tube anchovy paste
¼   teaspoon black pepper
1   teaspoon hot sauce
Dash of salt
1   dozen raw oysters, shucked

In large skillet melt butter. Add celery leaves, parsley, onion and garlic powder; sauté. Add frozen spinach. Allow spinach to thaw; remove from heat. In medium bowl combine spinach mixture with Worcestershire sauce and next 5 ingredients, then purée. Layer greased ramekins or muffin pans with 1 tablespoon spinach mixture, 1 oyster and top with additional spinach mixture. Bake at 500 degrees for 15 minutes. Yields 12 appetizer servings.

note...

● *Shucked oysters are available in most grocery seafood sections.*

Thanksgiving Oysters

2   cups crumbled saltine crackers, divided
1   cup butter, cut into pats and divided
3   dozen raw oysters, divided
Hot sauce to taste
Worcestershire sauce to taste
Salt and pepper to taste
1   cup heavy cream
1   cup half-and-half

● *Dish may be prepared in advance before adding cream and half-and-half.*

In prepared baking dish layer ½ cup crackers, ⅓ butter pats and 12 oysters. Sprinkle with hot sauce, Worcestershire, salt and pepper. Repeat layers twice and top with remaining ½ cup crackers. Immediately before baking, top with cream and half-and-half. Cover and bake at 350 degrees for 25 to 30 minutes or until bubbly. Yields 8-10 servings.

Glazed Grilled Salmon Fillet

4   center cut (6 ounce) salmon fillets, skin removed
3   garlic cloves, minced
3   tablespoons low-sodium soy sauce
1/3   cup honey
3   tablespoons fresh lime juice
2   tablespoons Dijon mustard
Lime wedges

Place salmon in shallow dish and set aside. In small bowl mix garlic and next 4 ingredients; pour over salmon. Place plastic wrap directly on salmon and marinate at room temperature 15 minutes, turning salmon once or twice. Remove rack and preheat gas grill or build a charcoal fire. Spray grill rack with oil. When coals are glowing red, set rack about 3 inches above heat. Transfer salmon to grill and cook 5 to 6 minutes on each side, basting with marinade. Serve immediately with lime wedges. Yields 4 servings.

note...

Salmon may also be prepared by placing on foil-lined broiling pan lightly sprayed with nonstick cooking spray. Place pan 3 inches from heat and broil 5 to 6 minutes on each side.

Sautéed Salmon with Spinach

4   tablespoons extra virgin olive oil, divided
4   skinless, boneless (6-8 ounce) salmon fillets
1   bunch fresh spinach, washed
Salt and pepper to taste
1/2   cup chopped green onions
2-3   garlic cloves, minced
1/4   teaspoon freshly ground black pepper
1/2   teaspoon salt, divided
3   tomatoes peeled, seeded and cut into 1/2-inch pieces
1   tablespoon finely chopped parsley

Spoon 1 tablespoon olive oil over salmon in shallow dish or plate. Cover with plastic wrap and chill. Heat 1 tablespoon olive oil in skillet; sauté spinach 1 1/2 minutes. Season with salt and pepper to taste and transfer to four individual serving plates. Heat 2 tablespoons olive oil in skillet. Sauté onions and garlic 1 minute. Add tomatoes, pepper and 1/4 teaspoon salt. Cook 30 seconds and set aside. Heat skillet until very hot. Remove salmon from refrigerator and add 1/4 teaspoon salt. Sauté salmon 2 minutes on each side. Let salmon rest in skillet before serving. Spoon onion, garlic and tomato mixture over spinach and top with salmon. Sprinkle with parsley and serve. Yields 4 servings.

Grilled Salmon and Vegetable Salad

10	fillets (6 ounce) Norwegian salmon	2-3	tablespoons butter
2	zucchini	8	ounces goat cheese
2	yellow squash	1	head Bibb lettuce, washed and torn
3	carrots	1	bunch spinach, washed and torn
2	red bell peppers		Lemon slices, for garnish
2	green bell peppers		Sprigs of cilantro, for garnish
			Lemon Herb Dressing

Place salmon in shallow dish. Pour ½ cup dressing over fillets. Cover and chill at least 1 hour. Cut zucchini, squash, carrots and peppers into thick julienne strips. Combine and cover with ½ cup dressing, tossing well to coat, and chill at least 1 hour. Grill salmon approximately 5 to 6 minutes per side, or until fish flakes easily; cool slightly. Sauté vegetables in 2 to 3 tablespoons butter until crisp tender. Add goat cheese and toss over low heat until vegetables are coated. In large bowl toss spinach and Bibb lettuce with remaining dressing. Arrange on individual serving plates and top with vegetables and salmon fillets. Garnish with lemon slices and sprigs of cilantro. Yields 10 servings.

Lemon Herb Dressing:

1½ cups lemon juice		3	teaspoons paprika
1	cup vegetable oil	3	teaspoons dried basil
2	teaspoons cilantro, chopped	1	teaspoon seasoned salt
1	teaspoon garlic, minced	1	teaspoon pepper
2	tablespoons sugar		

Combine all ingredients in a jar. Shake to combine. Refrigerate.

Easy But Elegant Salmon en Papillote

½ cup olive oil
1 shallot, minced
2 garlic cloves
¼ cup fresh dill, minced
Juice of 1 lime
4 fillets (8 ounce) salmon, skin removed
Kosher salt to taste

Cut four 13x13 pieces of parchment paper or aluminum foil. Fold and trim each to a heart shape. In small bowl combine olive oil and next 4 ingredients; set aside. Arrange one fillet next to fold line on half of each parchment heart. Sprinkle fish with kosher salt and top with ¼ of olive oil mixture. Fold over other half of each parchment heart. Starting with rounded edge, fold, pleat and crimp edges together, continuing to point of heart in order to completely seal. Twist ends tightly to seal. Place on baking sheet and bake at 425 degrees for 15 minutes or until parchment is puffed and lightly browned. Place on individual serving plates and cut open. Serve immediately. Yields 4 servings.

Grilled Ponzu Marinated Salmon

4 salmon steaks (1½ inches thick)

Ponzu Marinade:
Juice of 1-2 limes
3-4 tablespoons soy sauce
1-2 teaspoons mirin (Japanese cooking wine) or dry sherry
Kosher salt and pepper to taste
2-3 tablespoons extra virgin olive oil
Freshly ground black pepper

Preheat grill. In glass dish combine lime juice, soy sauce, mirin and olive oil. Marinate salmon about 5 minutes on each side. Sprinkle lightly with kosher salt and pepper. Grill about 5 minutes on each side. Yields 4 servings.

Pine Nut Crusted Snapper

note...

Any firm fleshed white fish may be used in place of red snapper.

2   **slices white bread, torn into pieces**
1/4   **cup pine nuts, toasted**
1   **egg white, beaten**
1/4   **teaspoon salt**
1/8   **teaspoon pepper**
4   **fillets (6 ounce) red snapper**
2   **teaspoons butter, melted**
Lime wedges

Preheat oven to 400 degrees. Place bread in food processor and process until crumbs are fine. Add pine nuts and pulse until pine nuts are finely chopped. Place breadcrumb mixture in shallow dish; place egg white in shallow bowl. Sprinkle fish with salt and pepper. Dip in egg white, then coat in breadcrumb mixture. Place fish on baking sheet coated with nonstick cooking spray; drizzle butter over fish. Bake at 400 degrees for 15 minutes, or until outside is crisp and browned and fish flakes easily with fork. Serve with lime wedges. Yields 4 servings.

Vegetables & Condiments

No Cars
by John Cook

Notes...

- *Avoid storing carrots near apples. This will give the carrots a bitter taste.*
- *Asparagus stalks should be tender and firm. Tips should be closed and compact. The most tender stalks have very little white on them. Remember to use fresh asparagus immediately, since it toughens rapidly.*
- *Place onions in the freezer 15 minutes before slicing to eliminate the odor.*

Vegetables & Condiments

Picnic Green Beans 126

J.B.'s "Must-Try" Skinny Beans 126

German Style Black-Eyed Peas 127

The Best Brussels Sprouts with Bacon 128

Roasted Asparagus with Hot Crab Sauce 128

Cold Asparagus with Pecans 129

Spinach with Raisins and Pine Nuts 129

Broccoli Strudel 130

Zucchini au Gratin 131

Dill Cherry Tomatoes 131

Tomato Tart 132

Silky Corn Casserole 133

Brandied Mushroom Pie 133

Havarti and Corn Stuffed Chili Rellenos
with Walnut Cream Sauce 134

Carrot Soufflé 135

Cashew Salad Dressing 135

Creamy Parmesan, Basil and
Pine Nut Dressing 136

Best Vinaigrette 136

Tried and True Pesto 137

Dijon Mustard Sauce 137

Rémoulade Sauce 138

Bordelaise Sauce 138

Perini Ranch Steak Rub 139

All-Purpose Meat Marinade 139

Marinade for Pork Tenderloin and
Venison Backstrap 140

Port, Rosemary and Garlic Marinade 140

Crispy Dijon Marinade 141

Mom's Buttermilk Marinade 141

Tomato-Avocado Salsa 142

Mango Salsa 142

Mexican Relish 143

Pico de Gallo 143

Picnic Green Beans

note...

- *Best prepared the day before serving, allowing bean mixture to marinate.*

- *Will keep at least 4 days in the refrigerator.*

1	package (1 pound) French cut frozen green beans
3/4	cup white vinegar
1/4	cup tarragon vinegar
3/4	cup sugar
1/2	cup water
2	tablespoons cooking oil
1	cup thinly sliced purple onions
1	can (8 ounce) sliced water chestnuts, drained
1/4	teaspoon salt
1/4	teaspoon pepper

Cook green beans according to package directions. Drain well and set aside. Combine vinegars, sugar, water and oil and bring to a rolling boil. Combine green beans, onions and chestnuts in large bowl. Pour hot vinegar mixture over green bean mixture. Add salt and pepper, stirring gently. Cool and chill until ready to serve. Yields 8-10 servings.

J.B.'s "Must-Try" Skinny Beans

1/2	large onion, chopped
1	tablespoon butter
2	cans (15 ounce) black beans, drained and rinsed
2	cans (15 ounce) whole kernel corn, drained
1	can (15 ounce) diced tomatoes
1 1/2	teaspoons cumin
4	tablespoons barbecue sauce
	Salt and pepper to taste
	Cooked white rice

In Dutch oven sauté onion in butter until tender. Add black beans and next 5 ingredients and cook slowly for 30 to 40 minutes. Serve over rice. Yields 6-8 servings.

German Style Black-Eyed Peas

1	package (16 ounce) dried black-eyed peas		1	carrot, sliced
3	cups chicken broth		1	celery stalk, sliced
1/2-1	pound Kielbasa sausage, thinly sliced		3	garlic cloves, minced
			Salt and pepper to taste	
3	tablespoons butter		1	teaspoon dried basil
1	medium onion, chopped		1	teaspoon dried dill

Soak black-eyed peas in water (enough to cover) in Dutch oven overnight. Drain and rinse peas; add chicken broth and sausage to peas. Melt butter in skillet and sauté onion, carrot and celery; add garlic. Combine with pea mixture. Add salt, pepper, basil and dill. Simmer 3 hours on low heat. Yields 6-8 servings.

The Best Brussels Sprouts with Bacon

3 cups fresh Brussels sprouts, or 2 packages frozen, thawed
1/2 cup onion, finely diced
3-4 bacon slices, diced
2 tablespoons olive oil
Salt and freshly ground black pepper
1/3 cup white wine

Cut out Brussels sprout stems and separate into leaves or thinly slice. Sauté onion and bacon in olive oil. Pour off fat, reserving 2-3 tablespoons. Add sprout leaves to pan, sauté, season with salt and moisten with a little white wine. Cover and simmer 10 to 15 minutes until tender. Season with pepper and serve. Yields 4-6 servings.

Roasted Asparagus with Hot Crab Sauce

Roasted Asparagus:
2   **pounds thick fresh asparagus**
2   **tablespoons olive oil**
Kosher salt to taste
Freshly ground black pepper to taste
Hot Crab Sauce
¼   **cup slivered almonds, toasted**

Preheat oven to 375 degrees. Wash and pat dry asparagus. On a large baking sheet, drizzle with oil; sprinkle with kosher salt and pepper to taste. Roast 10 to 15 minutes, depending upon thickness of asparagus. Asparagus should just be tender. Divide asparagus among individual serving plates. Spoon Hot Crab Sauce over each serving and top with almonds. Serve immediately. Yields 4-6 servings.

Hot Crab Sauce:
2   **packages (8 ounce) cream cheese**
¼   **cup mayonnaise**
⅓   **cup dry white wine**
1   **teaspoon sugar**
1   **teaspoon prepared mustard**
½   **teaspoon onion juice**
¼   **teaspoon garlic salt or to taste**
⅛   **teaspoon seasoned salt or to taste**
1   **can (9 ounce) crabmeat, drained and rinsed**

In large saucepan over low heat, blend cream cheese and next 7 ingredients until smooth. Stir in crab, breaking up large chunks. Cook in double boiler or over very low flame until hot. Sauce may be prepared ahead and reheated.

Cold Asparagus with Pecans

1½ pounds fresh asparagus
1   red bell pepper, thinly sliced
¾   cup pecans, finely chopped
2   tablespoons cooking oil
¼   cup cider vinegar
¼   cup soy sauce
¼   cup sugar
Salt and pepper

In medium saucepan plunge asparagus in boiling water 2 minutes. Drain and rinse under ice water to stop cooking process. Arrange asparagus in 1 to 2 layers in serving dish. In mixing bowl combine red bell pepper and next 5 ingredients; pour over asparagus, lifting so mixture penetrates to bottom. Sprinkle with salt and pepper and serve chilled. Yields 6 servings.

note...
May be prepared one day in advance.

Spinach with Raisins and Pine Nuts

⅔   cup golden raisins
6   pounds fresh spinach, coarse stems discarded
4   tablespoons extra virgin olive oil
4   garlic cloves, minced
1   teaspoon salt
⅔   cup toasted pine nuts

Soak raisins in warm water for 10 minutes. Drain and set aside. Thoroughly wash spinach. Steam spinach over medium-high heat until leaves are tender (about 2 to 3 minutes). Drain, cool and pat dry. Heat olive oil in large skillet over medium heat. Add garlic and sauté until garlic begins to turn opaque. Add spinach and cook, stirring frequently, 1 minute. Stir in salt, pine nuts and raisins. Continue to cook 3 minutes. Serve immediately. Yields 6-8 servings.

Broccoli Strudel

note...

When working with phyllo dough, thaw per package instructions. Unroll thawed dough on the counter. Cover lightly with a damp cloth at all times to prevent drying and cracking.

½ cup sliced green onions	2 tablespoons chopped parsley
2 garlic cloves, minced	1 carton (16 ounce)
2 tablespoons butter, divided	1% small curd cottage cheese
1¼ pounds broccoli	3 tablespoons pesto sauce
½ teaspoon salt	¾ cup Parmesan cheese
2½ ounces boiled	1 cup butter
deli-style ham, diced	20 sheets frozen phyllo dough, thawed
3 egg yolks, beaten	½ cup breadcrumbs, divided

Preheat oven to 350 degrees. In medium skillet sauté green onions and garlic in 1 tablespoon butter and set aside. Remove and discard lower 3 inches of tough broccoli stems. In large saucepan add salt to boiling water; cook broccoli several minutes until bright green, yet still crisp. Drain and chop cooked broccoli into ½-inch chunks. In large bowl combine broccoli, green onion mixture, ham and next 6 ingredients. Mix well and set aside. In small saucepan melt 1 cup butter. Unroll phyllo dough and cover with a damp cloth. Lift 1 phyllo sheet to a cutting board. Brush with melted butter. Sprinkle with 1 teaspoon breadcrumbs. Place second phyllo sheet over first. Brush with butter and sprinkle with 1 teaspoon breadcrumbs. Repeat until 5 phyllo sheets are stacked. Spread one-fourth of broccoli mixture across short end and down 3 inches from the top. Starting at top of short end, roll sheets into cylinder. Brush with remaining 1 tablespoon melted butter. Place on baking sheet, seam side down. Cut 3 to 4 slits in top to let strudel vent while baking. Repeat procedure with remaining phyllo and broccoli mixture. Bake for 25 minutes or until golden brown. Cool before slicing. Yields 4 (16 ounce) strudels.

Zucchini au Gratin

2   tablespoons olive oil
4   zucchini, sliced
1   large onion, sliced
12 ounces mozzarella or Monterey Jack cheese, shredded
1/2 cup Parmesan cheese
1/2 cup freshly minced parsley
Salt and pepper
1/2 cup fresh breadcrumbs
1/4 cup butter, sliced

Preheat oven to 350 degrees. Pour olive oil into a 9x13 baking dish. Layer half of zucchini, onion, mozzarella, Parmesan and parsley. Lightly season with salt and pepper. Repeat layers. Top with breadcrumbs and dot with butter. Bake, uncovered, for 40 minutes. Yields 6 servings.

Dill Cherry Tomatoes

1   tablespoon butter
1/2 teaspoon salt
1/2 teaspoon pepper
1/4 teaspoon garlic powder
1   teaspoon fresh dill or 1/4 teaspoon dried dill
2   dozen cherry tomatoes

Melt butter in skillet. Add salt, pepper, garlic powder and dill. Add tomatoes and cook just a few minutes, coating well with dill sauce. Yields 4-6 servings.

note...
Don't overcook or tomato skins will crack; tomatoes should be firm.

Tomato Tart

1	cup heavy cream	1/4	teaspoon ground white pepper
1/2	cup half-and-half	2	(9-inch) pie shells
2	eggs	4	tomatoes, sliced 1/2-inch thick
2	egg yolks	2	tablespoons chopped basil
1 1/2	cups Tomato Purée	1/2	cup shredded Swiss cheese
1/2	teaspoon salt	1/2	cup shredded Parmesan cheese

Preheat oven to 375 degrees. Make tomato purée. Blend heavy cream and next 6 ingredients in blender until frothy. Fill pie shells with mixture. Arrange tomato slices in a circle slightly overlapping on top of the mixture. Sprinkle with chopped basil and cheeses. Transfer tarts to baking sheet and bake for 35 minutes, or until filling is set and tomatoes have cooked but not wilted. Serve hot. Yields 6-8 servings.

Tomato Purée:

4-5	tomatoes, quartered and seeded	1	bay leaf
1	medium onion, quartered	2	tablespoons butter
Parsley sprig		1/2	teaspoon salt
1/4	teaspoon thyme	1/4	teaspoon pepper
		Pinch of sugar	

Place tomatoes in blender and blend 10 seconds. Transfer to bowl and set aside. Place onion in blender and blend 10 seconds, or until onion is minced. Add parsley, thyme and bay leaf and blend 2 seconds. Heat butter in heavy skillet; add tomatoes and onion mixture. Stir briefly; add salt, pepper and pinch of sugar. Cover and cook mixture over low heat 10 minutes. Remove cover and stir with wooden spoon, continuing to cook over a high heat 4 minutes until a thick paste forms. Yields 1 1/2 to 2 cups.

Silky Corn Casserole

1	tablespoon butter	1/2	teaspoon salt
1/2	cup sliced green onions	1/4	teaspoon red pepper flakes
2 1/4	cups milk	1/3	cup, plus 1 tablespoon all-purpose flour
1	tablespoon, plus 1 teaspoon sugar	4	eggs, lightly beaten
		3 1/2	cups corn, cut from cob (about 7 ears)

Melt butter in saucepan over medium heat. Add green onions and sauté 1 minute. Add milk, sugar, salt and red pepper flakes; cook 3 minutes or until hot, being careful not to boil. Remove from heat and set aside. Combine flour and eggs in bowl; beat at medium speed with an electric mixer until well blended. Gradually stir in 1/2 cup hot milk mixture. Stir in corn; pour into lightly oiled shallow 2-quart casserole dish. Bake at 350 degrees for 1 hour, 20 minutes or until a knife inserted in center comes out clean. Yields 6 servings.

Brandied Mushroom Pie

1/2	cup butter	1/2	cup half-and-half
2	medium onions, chopped	1	tablespoon cognac
1	pound large mushrooms, sliced		Salt and pepper to taste
			Pastry for 1 (9-inch) double pie crust
1	tablespoon flour	1	egg, beaten and diluted with a little water

Preheat oven to 450 degrees. Heat butter in skillet and sauté onion until transparent. Add mushrooms and cook 5 minutes, stirring occasionally. Stir in flour and half-and-half, continuing to stir until mixture boils. Stir in cognac, salt and pepper; let cool. Line a pie plate with pastry crust. Spoon cooled mushroom mixture into pie plate. Cut second crust into 1/2-inch strips. Arrange pastry strips in lattice pattern, pressing ends to edge and fluting with fingertips. Lightly brush pastry with egg mixture. Bake on lowest oven rack for 20 minutes or until crust is brown. Yields 6-8 servings.

Havarti and Corn Stuffed Chile Rellenos with Walnut Cream Sauce

Rellenos:
10 large poblano peppers
1½ cups shredded Monterey Jack cheese
1½ cups shredded Havarti cheese
6   ears of corn, cooked and kernels cut from cob

Place whole peppers on an aluminum foil-lined baking sheet; broil 5 inches from heat (with electric oven door partially open) about 5 minutes on each side or until peppers look blistered. Place roasted peppers in a heavy-duty, plastic freezer bag immediately; seal and let stand 10 minutes. Peel peppers; slit open and remove seeds, keeping peppers intact. Set aside. In medium bowl combine shredded cheeses and corn, mixing well. Fill peppers with cheese mixture and flatten. Place peppers on baking sheet coated with nonstick cooking spray. Bake at 350 degrees until cheese is bubbly. Serve Walnut Cream Sauce over warm poblanos. Yields 10 servings.

Walnut Cream Sauce:
1   package (8 ounce) cream cheese, softened
⅓ cup milk
½ cup walnuts

Place cream cheese in food processor and process until smooth and creamy. Add milk a little at a time to create consistency. Add walnuts and process until nuts are minced. Warm in double boiler.

Carrot Soufflé

1	pound carrots, peeled and sliced
1/2	cup butter, melted
3	eggs
1	cup sugar
3	tablespoons flour
1	teaspoon baking powder
1	teaspoon vanilla

Cook carrots in a small amount of boiling, salted water until tender; drain. Combine carrots and butter in blender and blend until smooth. Add eggs and remaining ingredients and blend well. Spoon mixture into lightly oiled 1-quart casserole or soufflé dish. Bake at 350 degrees for 45 minutes or until firm. Yields 8 servings.

Cashew Salad Dressing

1 1/2	cups cooking oil
3/4	cup water
1/2	cup honey
4 1/2	teaspoons dill
3	teaspoons light soy sauce
3/4	cup chopped cashews
1/3	cup white vinegar
3	tablespoons lemon juice
3	garlic cloves, minced

Blend all ingredients in blender or food processor and refrigerate. Shake well before serving. Yields dressing for 1 large or 2 small salads.

note...

To enhance flavor of dressing, prepare one day in advance.

Creamy Parmesan, Basil and Pine Nut Dressing

2   tablespoons Parmesan cheese, grated
4   tablespoons fresh basil leaves
1   tablespoon toasted pine nuts
2½ teaspoons minced garlic
1   shallot, peeled and chopped
⅓   cup olive oil (preferably basil-infused)
2½ tablespoons champagne or balsamic vinegar

In food processor or blender, purée Parmesan and next 4 ingredients. Slowly add olive oil, processing continuously. Add champagne or balsamic vinegar and pulse to combine. Refrigerate until serving. Yields dressing for 4 servings.

note...

Best if made just prior to serving.

Best Vinaigrette

½   tablespoon coarse grain Dijon mustard
4   tablespoons rice wine vinegar
1   teaspoon sugar
½   teaspoon salt
½   teaspoon freshly ground black pepper
1   teaspoon chopped chives
½   cup olive oil

Whisk together mustard and next 5 ingredients. Continue whisking mixture while gradually adding oil until mixture thickens. Adjust seasonings to taste. Serve over greens immediately. Yields 1 cup.

Crispy Dijon Marinade

6	shallots	3	tablespoons dried thyme leaves
6	garlic cloves, peeled	1	tablespoon kosher salt
½	cup butter, melted		Freshly ground black pepper
1	jar (9 ounce) Dijon mustard	3	slices bread, processed, optional
¼	cup olive oil	¼	cup Parmesan cheese, grated, optional
½-1	teaspoon red pepper flakes		

Process shallots and garlic in food processor. Add butter, mustard and oil and process. Add pepper flakes, thyme, salt and pepper. Rub marinade over birds, reserving some marinade. Refrigerate overnight. Yields 2 cups.

Optional: Before cooking, rub birds again with marinade. Process bread, Parmesan and additional pinch of thyme and pepper flakes. Pat on breadcrumb mixture. Spray with nonstick cooking spray and bake accordingly.

Marinade for:
6-8 Cornish game hens; Bake at 350 degrees for 25 to 40 minutes or until done.
10 chicken breasts; Bake at 350 degrees for 20 to 30 minutes.
10-12 quail; Bake at 350 degrees for 20 to 30 minutes.

Mom's Buttermilk Marinade

1	cup buttermilk	1	tablespoon salt-free seasoning blend
1	cup Dijon mustard	5	teaspoons minced garlic
½	cup Italian dressing	5	tablespoons olive oil
1	tablespoon thyme		Juice of 2 lemons
1	teaspoon oregano		Freshly cracked black pepper to taste
1	tablespoon Italian seasoning		

Combine all ingredients. Pour over 10 chicken pieces with skin. Chill overnight before grilling. Grill 20-30 minutes or until done. Yields 10 servings.

Tomato-Avocado Salsa

6   plum tomatoes, peeled, seeded and chopped
1   garlic clove, finely chopped
1   red bell pepper, seeded and finely chopped
1   jalapeño pepper, seeded and finely chopped
1   medium red onion, finely chopped
1   avocado, pitted, peeled and chopped
1/2 cup tightly packed cilantro leaves
Juice of 2 limes
Salt and pepper to taste

Combine all ingredients and chill 1 to 2 hours. Serve with chips, or as an accompaniment to grilled fish or chicken. Yields 4 cups (16 servings).

Mango Salsa

1   mango, peeled and chopped
1   cup mild, medium or hot salsa
1   tablespoon fresh lime juice
1/4 teaspoon cumin
1/4 cup fresh chopped cilantro

Combine all ingredients, mixing well. Chill until ready to serve. Yields 6-8 servings.

Mexican Relish

1	can (15 ounce) black beans, drained and rinsed		1	bunch green onions, chopped
1	can (15 ounce) sweet corn kernels, drained		1/3	cup chopped green olives
2	medium tomatoes, chopped		2	tablespoons chopped pickled jalapeños
1/2	cup chopped fresh cilantro		1	tablespoon juice from jalapeño jar
			1/2	cup rice vinegar

Combine all ingredients, mixing well. Yields 6-8 servings.

note...

Relish may be served as a dip or as a sauce for fajitas or other meats.

Pico de Gallo

4-6	tomatoes, chopped		1	tablespoon olive oil
1-1½	onions, chopped		1	tablespoon sugar
4	garlic cloves, minced		1	tablespoon salt or to taste
3-5	jalapeño peppers, chopped		4	tablespoons washed, dried and chopped cilantro
½-1	cup chopped jicama			
2-3	tablespoons lime juice			

Combine all ingredients. Prepare at least an hour before serving or a day in advance. Yields 6-8 servings.

Pasta, Rice & Potatoes

Notre Dame
by John Cook

sponsored by
JIM AND DEEDEE LEE
BRUCE AND MARIA BUDNER

Notes...

- *A large, heavy pot with a tight fitting lid may be used in place of a Dutch oven.*
- *To make rice fluffier and drier, place a slice of dry bread on top of it after cooking. Cover for 10 minutes. Remove bread and fluff with a fork.*
- *Keep boiled potatoes white by adding a teaspoon of lemon juice or vinegar to the cooking water.*

Pasta, Rice & Potatoes

Lasagna Roll-Ups 146

Angel Hair with
Red Pepper-Lime Purée. 146

Pasta Timbales. 147

Simply Delicious Bow Tie Pasta with
Garlic and Basil 147

Italian Meat Sauce for a Crowd 148

Winter Night Spaghetti with
Sausage and Sage 148

Summer Pasta with
Vine Ripe Tomatoes and Basil 149

Penne Mediterraneo Salad 149

Paella Salad 150

"Best-Ever" Rice 150

Oregano Rice 151

Cumin Rice 151

Herbed Wild Rice with Toasted Pine Nuts . . . 152

Herbed Couscous with Feta 152

Polenta, Tomato and Pesto Casserole 153

Fast and Easy Polenta with
Roasted Vegetables 154

Louisiana Grits 155

Decadent But Delicious Cheese Grits 155

Spinach Spoonbread 156

Corn-Potato Pancakes 156

Citrus Baked New Potatoes 157

Gruyère Potato Gratin 157

Whipped Potatoes with a Twist 158

Sliced Baked Potatoes 158

Savory Sweet Potato Gratin 159

Holiday Sweet Potatoes 160

Lasagna Roll-Ups

1 pound ground beef or
ground turkey breast
1 onion, chopped
2 garlic cloves, minced
2 cans (15 ounce)
Italian style tomato sauce
1 teaspoon dried basil
1 teaspoon dried oregano
2 cups non-fat or
low-fat ricotta or cottage cheese

1/2 cup shredded mozzarella cheese
2 tablespoons Parmesan cheese
1 package (10 ounce) chopped spinach,
thawed and drained
1/2 teaspoon black pepper
1 package (8 ounce) wide lasagna noodles,
cooked and drained

Brown beef, onion and garlic in large skillet. Add tomato sauce, basil and oregano and simmer 30 minutes on low. Spread 1/2 of sauce into bottom of a 12-inch x 7-inch baking dish and set aside. To prepare filling, combine cheeses, spinach and pepper. Spread each noodle with 1/2 cup filling; roll and place seam side down in baking dish. Spoon remaining 1/2 of sauce over lasagna rolls. Cover with foil and bake at 375 degrees for 45 minutes. Yields 6-8 servings.

Angel Hair with Red Pepper-Lime Purée

6 red bell peppers, roasted,
seeded and chopped
1 teaspoon chopped garlic
1/4 cup cilantro, chopped
1/4 cup lime juice

1/2 teaspoon cayenne pepper
Salt to taste
2 tablespoons olive oil
1 pound angel hair pasta, cooked al dente
1/2 cup grated Parmesan cheese

In food processor purée peppers and next 5 ingredients. Transfer purée to large skillet and sauté in oil about 5 minutes. Toss with pasta and sprinkle with Parmesan. Yields 4 servings.

Pasta Timbales

Butter
1¾ cups grated Parmesan cheese,
    divided
1¼ cups crème fraîche
1¼ cups ricotta
1¼ cups half-and-half

4   eggs
2   teaspoons salt
½   teaspoon freshly ground white pepper
½   cup fresh basil leaves
1   pound fresh spinach fettuccine, cooked

Generously butter muffin tins. Sprinkle 1 teaspoon Parmesan cheese into each cup, tilting pan to distribute evenly. Blend ½ cup Parmesan, crème fraîche and next 5 ingredients in food processor. Blend in basil. Spoon 2 tablespoons cheese mixture into each cup. Mound pasta into each cup. Top each cup with remaining cheese mixture, filling almost to top. Sprinkle ½ teaspoon Parmesan over each cup. Freeze until firm (at least 2 hours). Cover with foil and return to freezer. (Timbales may be prepared 1 week in advance to this point.) Position rack in lower third of oven and preheat to 375 degrees. Bake frozen timbales, uncovered, for 35 minutes or until bottoms are light brown. (Tops should not be dry.) Loosen from cups by running sharp knife around sides. Yields 24-36 timbales.

Simply Delicious Bow Tie Pasta with Garlic and Basil

1   package (12 ounce)
    bow tie pasta
20 fresh basil leaves,
    finely chopped
4   garlic cloves, crushed

½   teaspoon salt
⅓   cup grated Parmesan cheese
¼   cup olive oil
3   tablespoons lemon juice

Cook bow tie pasta according to package directions. Drain, rinse and set aside. Mix basil with garlic, salt and Parmesan. Toss basil mixture with pasta and set aside. Whisk a small stream of lemon juice into oil until well blended. Add oil mixture to pasta, stirring carefully to blend all ingredients. Chill until ready to serve. Yields 6 servings.

Italian Meat Sauce for a Crowd

note...

- *Additional cans of tomato sauce or chopped tomatoes may be added to taste.*

2   **pounds ground round**
Olive oil
1   **green bell pepper, seeded and chopped**
1   **large onion, chopped**
6-8 **garlic cloves, chopped**
5   **cans (15 ounce) tomato sauce**
1   **can (14½) chopped tomatoes**

1   **can (6 ounce) tomato paste**
4   **bay leaves, crushed**
8   **tablespoons oregano**
3-4 **tablespoons rosemary**
4   **tablespoons basil**
Salt and pepper to taste
2-3 **tablespoons brown sugar, optional**

In a Dutch oven brown ground round in olive oil. Add bell pepper, onion and garlic and cook until tender. Add tomato sauce, tomatoes and tomato paste to meat mixture. Cook slowly on low heat, stirring occasionally. Add bay leaves, oregano, rosemary, basil, salt and pepper to taste. (Sugar may be added if a sweeter sauce is preferred.) Cook slowly on low heat for at least 1 hour. Serve over pasta. Sauce freezes well. Yields 14-16 servings.

Winter Night Spaghetti with Sausage and Sage

- *If desired, Italian plum tomatoes may be broken by cutting them slightly with kitchen shears while still in the can.*

1   **tablespoon olive oil**
1   **onion, chopped coarsely**
4   **garlic cloves, chopped coarsely**
1   **package (16 ounce) bulk sausage**
1   **bunch sage leaves, chopped or 1½ teaspoons dried sage**
1   **teaspoon red pepper flakes, or to taste**

1   **teaspoon salt**
½   **teaspoon pepper**
1   **carton fresh button mushrooms, sliced**
1   **can (14½ ounce) whole Italian plum tomatoes**
1   **pound spaghetti, cooked and drained**
Parmesan cheese to taste

Heat olive oil in large heavy pot or skillet. Add onion and garlic and sauté quickly until tender. Add sausage, breaking up to brown. Add sage, red pepper flakes, salt and pepper. Add mushrooms and sauté lightly. Add tomatoes, breaking up with a spoon. Reduce heat and simmer to allow flavors to blend. Add water if sauce becomes too thick. Toss spaghetti with sauce. Top with Parmesan cheese. Yields 6 servings.

Summer Pasta with Vine Ripened Tomatoes and Basil

5   vine-ripened tomatoes,
cut in 1-inch chunks

2-3   tablespoons kosher salt,
divided

1/2-3/4   pound Brie or Camembert
(rind removed), cubed

1   cup fresh basil leaves,
washed and chopped

1/3-1/2   cup extra virgin olive oil

1/2   teaspoon freshly ground
black pepper

2-4   garlic cloves, minced

1   pound linguine, penne,
bow tie or shell pasta

Freshly grated Parmesan cheese

1/2-1   teaspoon red pepper flakes,
optional

note...

- Use only the best, most flavorful summer tomatoes.

- Two pints of flavorful cherry tomatoes may be cut in half and substituted for the large tomatoes.

At least 2 hours before serving, combine tomatoes, 1 teaspoon kosher salt and next 5 ingredients. Combine well and cover with plastic wrap. Set out at room temperature until ready to serve. About 30 minutes before serving, fill large pot with water (about 6 quarts) and bring to a boil; add remaining salt. Boil pasta according to package directions. Remove pasta from water and drain, reserving 1/4 cup pasta water if needed. *Do not rinse pasta.* Immediately add pasta to tomato mixture and toss until cheese melts. If necessary, add reserved pasta water, 1 tablespoon at a time, to thin the sauce. Serve with Parmesan cheese and red pepper flakes, if desired. Yields 6-8 servings.

Penne Mediterraneo Salad

3/4   pound penne pasta,
cooked al dente,
rinsed and drained

1/4   cup pine nuts,
lightly toasted

2   roasted red peppers

1/2   cup sliced kalamata olives

1/4   cup chopped sun-dried tomatoes,
packed in oil

1/4   cup chopped fresh basil

2   tablespoons capers, rinsed and drained

2   tablespoons oil from sun-dried tomatoes

2   smoked chicken breasts, shredded

1/2   cup freshly shredded Parmesan cheese

In large bowl combine all ingredients, tossing well. Chill until ready to serve. Yields 4 servings.

Paella Salad

2	packages (5 ounce) saffron-flavored yellow rice	1	can (14 ounce) quartered artichoke hearts, drained
1/4	cup balsamic vinegar	3/4	cup chopped green bell pepper
1/4	cup lemon juice	1	cup frozen green peas, thawed
1	tablespoon olive oil	1	cup chopped tomato
1	teaspoon dried basil	1	jar (2 ounce) diced pimientos, drained
1/8	teaspoon black pepper	1/2	cup chopped red onion
Dash of cayenne pepper		2	ounce chopped prosciutto
1	pound medium shrimp, cooked and peeled		

Prepare rice according to package directions, omitting any oil or salt; set aside. In small bowl combine vinegar and next 5 ingredients; set aside. In large bowl combine rice, shrimp and remaining ingredients, mixing well. Pour vinegar dressing over rice mixture, tossing well to coat. Cover and chill at least 2 hours before serving. Yields 6 servings.

"Best-Ever" Rice

note...

Best-Ever Rice *freezes well. Thaw, add 3 tablespoons of water and heat in microwave in covered dish.*

1	onion, chopped
2	tablespoons olive oil
2	cups Texmati or jasmine rice, uncooked
2 1/2	cups chicken broth
1/2	cup chopped cilantro

Sauté onions in olive oil in large skillet 5 minutes. Add rice and sauté 3 minutes, stirring often. Add chicken broth and cilantro; bring to a boil. Cover and reduce heat to low; cook 15 minutes. Stir and serve immediately. Yields 6-8 servings.

Oregano Rice

4   green onions, chopped (tops included)
1   cup uncooked long grain rice
1/4 cup butter
2   cans (4 1/2 ounce) mushrooms
2   cans (10 1/2 ounce) beef broth
1/2 cup water
2   teaspoons oregano
Salt and pepper to taste

Preheat oven to 350 degrees. In large skillet sauté onions and rice in butter until rice begins to turn brown. Drain 1 can mushrooms. Add mushrooms, juice from 1 can and remaining ingredients. Remove from heat, transfer to baking dish and place in oven. Cover and bake for 45 minutes to 1 hour. Yields 6 servings.

note...
The use of light butter is not recommended.

Cumin Rice

1/3 cup chopped onion
1/4 cup chopped green bell pepper
1   cup uncooked long grain rice
2   tablespoons bacon drippings
2   cans (10 1/2 ounce) consommé
1   tablespoon Worcestershire sauce
3/4 teaspoon salt
3/4 teaspoon cumin seed

In large saucepan sauté onions, pepper and rice in bacon drippings on medium heat until golden brown. Add consommé, Worcestershire sauce, salt and cumin seed. Cover with tightly fitting lid and bring to a boil. When steam escapes, reduce to low and cook 20 minutes. Yields 6 servings.

Herbed Wild Rice with Toasted Pine Nuts

2   packages (6 ounce) long-grain and wild rice mix, *not* instant rice mix
2   tablespoons cooking oil
4   cups water
1   cup currants or golden raisins
1/2 cup cilantro leaves, chopped
1/2 cup basil leaves, chopped
1/2 cup pine nuts

Toast pine nuts until lightly toasted, watching carefully. In large skillet sauté rice in hot oil. Add seasoning packets, water and currants or raisins. Bring to a boil and cook 20 to 25 minutes. Remove from heat and steam covered for 5 minutes. Add cilantro, basil and pine nuts. Serve immediately. Yields 8-10 servings.

note...

Herbed Couscous with Feta may be prepared up to 6 hours in advance. Cover and chill; bring to room temperature before serving.

Herbed Couscous with Feta

3   cups water
2   cups couscous
2/3 cup freshly squeezed lemon juice
3   tablespoons red wine vinegar
2   tablespoons Dijon mustard
4   garlic cloves, minced
3/4 cup olive oil
1   bunch green onions, chopped
1   cucumber, peeled, seeded and chopped

1   can (3.8 ounce) sliced black olives, drained
1/2 cup parsley, chopped
1/4 cup chopped fresh mint leaves
1   can (15 ounce) garbanzo beans, drained and rinsed
2   packages (4 ounce) crumbled feta cheese

Bring water to a boil in heavy large saucepan. Mix in couscous. Cover and remove from heat. Let stand 10 minutes. Transfer couscous to large bowl; fluff with fork and set aside. Mix lemon juice, vinegar, mustard and garlic in small bowl; whisk in oil. Add lemon juice mixture, green onions and next 5 ingredients to couscous, tossing well. Add cheese and toss gently. Yields 8-10 servings.

Polenta, Tomato and Pesto Casserole

4   cups milk
1   tablespoon unsalted butter
1   teaspoon sugar
1/2-1 teaspoon salt
1⅓   cups stone-ground yellow cornmeal
1/2   cup Parmesan cheese, grated
2/3   cup ready-made basil pesto, divided
1   package (12 ounce) grated mozzarella cheese, divided
2-3 large tomatoes, sliced 1/2-inch thick

Preheat oven to 375 degrees. Combine milk, butter, sugar and salt in a heavy saucepan and heat just to a simmer. Slowly add the cornmeal in a thin stream, whisking constantly. Reduce heat and continue stirring with a wooden spoon until mixture has thickened and leaves the sides of the pan (about 10 minutes). Remove from heat and stir in Parmesan cheese. Immediately pour half of cornmeal mixture into prepared 7x11-inch baking pan or 2½-quart casserole. Work quickly before polenta stiffens and becomes difficult to spread. Top with half of pesto, spreading evenly over surface. Sprinkle with half of mozzarella. Top with tomato slices. If remaining polenta has cooled and is too thick to spread, whisk in a little hot milk. Pour remaining polenta over tomato layer. Spread polenta with a knife to reach edges of pan. Cover polenta surface with remaining pesto and sprinkle with remaining mozzarella. Bake for 30 minutes or until bubbling. Casserole may also be covered and chilled overnight; bake for 40 minutes at 375 degrees when ready to serve. Place casserole under broiler for a few minutes to brown top. Let stand 10 minutes before serving. Yields 8 servings.

Fast and Easy Polenta with Roasted Vegetables

4   cups chopped zucchini (about 5 small zucchini)
2$\frac{1}{2}$ cups chopped red bell pepper (about 2 peppers)
1   cup chopped red onion
3   tablespoons olive oil, divided
$\frac{1}{3}$ cup fresh basil, chopped
1$\frac{1}{2}$ tablespoons balsamic vinegar
$\frac{1}{4}$ teaspoon black pepper, divided
2   tubes (16 ounce) ready-made polenta, each cut crosswise into 12 slices
$\frac{1}{4}$ teaspoon salt
$\frac{1}{2}$ cup crumbled goat cheese (2 ounce)
Basil sprigs, for garnish

Preheat oven to 475 degrees. Combine zucchini, bell pepper, onion and 1 tablespoon olive oil in large bowl, tossing well to coat. Arrange in a single layer on a jelly-roll pan coated with nonstick cooking spray. Bake for 25 minutes or until tender, stirring after 15 minutes. Stir in basil, vinegar and 1/8 teaspoon black pepper. While vegetables roast, heat large skillet. Spray with nonstick cooking spray and add remaining 2 tablespoons olive oil to heat. Sprinkle polenta slices with salt and pepper. Sauté quickly to brown lightly on each side. (Polenta may also be prepared by browning slices under broiler 5 minutes on each side.) To serve, place polenta slices on each plate. Spoon roasted vegetables over polenta and sprinkle with cheese. Garnish with basil. Yields 6-8 servings.

Louisiana Grits

1½ cups grits
6   cups water
½   cup butter, cubed
3   teaspoons pepper blend
½   pound boxed processed cheese product, cubed
½   pound sharp Cheddar cheese, shredded
3   eggs, beaten
½   cup onion, browned
2   tablespoons pimiento, chopped
½   teaspoon salt

Cook grits in water according to package directions. Add remaining ingredients. Blend together and place in prepared baking dish. Bake, uncovered, at 350 degrees for 1 hour. If not serving immediately, bake covered and let stand. Yields 8 servings.

Decadent but Delicious Cheese Grits

8   cups heavy cream
1   teaspoon salt
1   teaspoon garlic powder
1   teaspoon pepper
2   cups quick cooking grits, uncooked
1   package (8 ounce) cream cheese, cubed
2   cups shredded Monterey Jack cheese
1   teaspoon hot sauce

In Dutch oven or large pot bring heavy cream, salt, garlic powder and pepper to a boil. Gradually stir in grits. Return to a boil; cover, reduce heat and simmer, stirring occasionally, 5 minutes or until thickened. Add cheeses and hot sauce, stirring until cheese melts. Yields 12 cups.

Spinach Spoonbread

2 tablespoons butter
2 tablespoons all-purpose flour
1 cup milk
Salt and pepper to taste
Paprika to taste
1 package (10 ounce) chopped
   spinach, cooked and drained

1 cup sour cream
2 eggs, beaten
1/2 cup melted butter
1 package (8 1/2 ounce) corn muffin mix

Preheat oven to 350 degrees. Melt 2 tablespoons butter in saucepan over low heat. Add flour to butter to make a roux; *Do not brown*. Gradually whisk in milk and stir until thickened. Add salt, pepper and paprika and set aside. Mix together spinach, sour cream, eggs and 1/2 cup melted butter. Add spinach mixture to white sauce. Add corn muffin mix, thoroughly combining. Pour into prepared 1 1/2-quart soufflé dish. Bake for 1 hour, uncovered. Yields 6-8 servings.

Corn-Potato Pancakes

1 package (16 ounce) frozen
   whole kernel corn, thawed
1 small onion, finely chopped
1/2 cup chopped green onions
2 teaspoons cooking oil
2 cups mashed potatoes

1/2 cup all-purpose flour
2 eggs, lightly beaten
3/4 teaspoon salt
1/2 teaspoon freshly ground pepper
Non-stick cooking spray
Salsa of choice

Sauté corn and onions in oil in large nonstick skillet over medium heat, stirring constantly, until crisp tender. Remove from heat and set aside. Combine mashed potatoes, flour and eggs, stirring well. Stir in corn mixture, salt and pepper. Coat a large skillet with cooking spray and place over medium heat until hot. Drop mixture by heaping tablespoons into skillet; cook 3 minutes on each side or until golden, wiping skillet as necessary. Drain and serve with salsa. Yields 14 pancakes.

Citrus Baked New Potatoes

3   pounds red skin new potatoes, washed and unpeeled
Salt and pepper to taste
3/4   cup butter, melted
1/2   cup freshly squeezed lemon juice
1 1/2 teaspoons crushed, dried thyme

Preheat oven to 375 degrees. Quarter potatoes and arrange in baking dish in single layer. Add salt and pepper. Combine butter and lemon juice and pour over potatoes. Sprinkle generously with thyme. Bake for 35 to 45 minutes. Yields 8 servings.

Gruyère Potato Gratin

3 1/2 pounds russet potatoes, peeled and cut into 1/8-inch thick slices
Salt and pepper to taste
3   tablespoons fresh dill, minced and divided
1   onion, thinly sliced and divided
3   cups shredded Gruyère cheese, divided (about 10 ounces)
1 1/3 cups heavy cream
1 1/3 cups chicken broth
1/4   cup Dijon mustard
1-2 garlic cloves, minced

Preheat oven to 400 degrees. Overlap 1/3 potatoes in lightly oiled 13x9x2-inch baking dish. Season generously with salt and pepper. Sprinkle with 1/2 teaspoon dill, 1/3 onion and 1 cup cheese. Repeat layering twice. Whisk cream, broth, mustard and garlic in bowl. Pour over potatoes. Bake about 1 hour or until tender and browned. Cool 10 minutes before serving. Yields 8-10 servings.

note...
Potatoes and onion may be sliced with a thin blade of mandolin or food processor.

Whipped Potatoes with a Twist

2   cups mashed potatoes
1   package (8 ounce) cream cheese, softened
1   onion, chopped
2   eggs, beaten
2   tablespoons all-purpose flour
Salt and pepper to taste
1   can (6 ounce) French fried onions

In large bowl combine potatoes and next 4 ingredients; season with salt and pepper. Top with French fried onions. Bake, uncovered, at 300 degrees for 35 minutes. Yields 6 servings.

Sliced Baked Potatoes

4   medium potatoes, uniformly shaped and washed
1   teaspoon salt
3   tablespoons butter, melted and divided
2   bunches green onions, chopped
1   cup cooked, crumbled bacon
1/2   cup shredded mozzarella or Cheddar cheese

Cut potatoes into thin slices, but do cut not all the way through. Place potatoes in baking dish and fan slightly. Sprinkle with salt and drizzle with 2 tablespoons butter. Bake at 425 degrees for 1 hour. Sauté green onions in remaining butter. Stuff potatoes between the slices with green onions, bacon and cheese. Bake for additional 15 minutes or until cheese melts. Yields 4 servings.

note...

- *Place a wooden spoon next to the potato. Slice to the handle to assure that you do not cut completely through the potato.*

- *For stuffing, use your imagination. Try sautéed mushrooms, spinach artichoke dip, crabmeat, etc.*

Savory Sweet Potato Gratin

3   tablespoons unsalted butter, divided
3-4 garlic cloves, minced
1   tablespoon all-purpose flour
1   cup heavy cream
4   sweet potatoes, peeled and sliced thin (about 2¼ pounds)
Salt and pepper to taste
10-12 fresh sage leaves, minced
½   cup breadcrumbs
½   cup freshly grated Parmesan cheese

Preheat oven to 325 degrees. In small skillet over low heat, melt 2 tablespoons butter and sauté garlic. Stir in flour and cook 3 minutes, stirring constantly. Stir in cream and bring mixture to a simmer, stirring occasionally. Arrange potatoes in layers in a well-buttered 1½-inch gratin dish, seasoning with salt, pepper and sage. Reserve ½ cup cream mixture and pour remaining cream mixture over potatoes. Bake for 1 hour or until tender. Remove from oven; baste top with reserved cream mixture and sprinkle with breadcrumbs. Melt remaining butter and drizzle on top. Bake for 15 minutes. Heat broiler; top potatoes with Parmesan cheese. Broil 1 to 2 minutes or until browned. Yields 6-8 servings.

note...
A mandolin or food processor may be used for uniform thin slices.

note...

So rich but so good!

8	sweet potatoes, peeled and cut in chunks
5	eggs
1	cup sugar
1	teaspoon cinnamon
$\frac{1}{2}$	teaspoon nutmeg
3	tablespoons vanilla
$\frac{1}{2}$	cup butter, melted

Boil potatoes until tender and drain. Blend together potatoes and remaining ingredients with an electric mixer. Transfer mixture to oiled baking pan. Bake at 350 degrees for 30 minutes.

Topping:

1	cup chopped pecans
$\frac{1}{4}$	cup butter, melted
$\frac{1}{4}$	cup flour

1-1$\frac{1}{2}$ cups brown sugar
Pinch of cinnamon
Pinch of nutmeg

Combine topping ingredients together in small bowl. Pour topping over potato mixture and bake at 350 degrees for 30 minutes. Watch carefully to see that pecans do not burn. Let cool about 15 minutes to allow for a crunchier topping. Yields 10-12 servings.

The Best Desserts

Oriental Quince
by John Cook

sponsored by

regency centers

Notes...

- *Just before icing a cake, dust a little cornstarch or flour on top to prevent the icing from running off.*
- *You get more volume from cakes if ingredients are at room temperature prior to mixing.*
- *Brown sugar won't harden if an apple slice is placed in the container. But if your brown sugar is already brick-hard, put your cheese grater to work and grate the amount you need.*
- *Keep cookies crisp by placing crushed tissue paper in the bottom of the cookie jar.*

Pecan Pie with Kahlúa and Chocolate Chips

1/2 cup sugar	1 cup chopped pecans
1/4 cup unsalted butter, softened	1/2 cup semi-sweet chocolate chips
1 tablespoon all-purpose flour	1 frozen (9-inch) deep-dish pie crust, unbaked
3/4 cup dark corn syrup	2/3 cup heavy cream, chilled
1/4 cup Kahlúa or other coffee liqueur	1/4 cup confectioners' sugar
1 teaspoon vanilla	1/2 teaspoon vanilla
3 eggs	Pecan halves, optional

Preheat oven to 375 degrees. Beat sugar and butter in medium bowl until smooth. Add flour, mixing well. Gradually add corn syrup, then Kahlúa and vanilla. Mix in eggs; fold in pecans. Sprinkle chocolate chips over bottom of crust. Pour filling over chocolate chips. Bake for 40-45 minutes or until filling is puffed around edges and just set in center. Transfer to wire rack and cool completely. Beat cream in medium bowl until peaks form. Add confectioners' sugar and vanilla. Beat until well mixed. Drop whipped cream in small dollops around edge of pie. Place pecan half atop each dollop, if desired. Yields 6-8 servings.

note...

- *When baking pie, cover edge of crust with foil if browning too quickly.*

- *Pie may be prepared 1 day in advance. Cover and chill.*

Praline Pumpkin Pie

1/3 cup finely ground pecans, firmly packed	1/4 teaspoon ground cloves
1 cup light brown sugar, firmly packed, divided	1/8 teaspoon mace
2 tablespoons butter, softened	1/2 teaspoon cinnamon
1 (9-inch) pie shell, unbaked	1/2 teaspoon ginger
2 eggs	1/2 teaspoon salt
1 cup canned pumpkin	1 cup heavy cream
1 tablespoon all-purpose flour	1/4 cup confectioners' sugar
	1/2 teaspoon vanilla

Preheat oven to 450 degrees. Combine pecans, 1/3 cup sugar and butter in small bowl. Press onto bottom of pie shell with back of spoon. Bake pie shell for 10 minutes. Combine remaining sugar, eggs and remaining ingredients and beat until creamy. Pour over praline layer in pie shell. Bake at 325 degrees for 45 minutes or until cake tester inserted in center comes out clean. Beat cream in medium bowl until peaks form. Add confectioners' sugar and vanilla. Beat until well mixed. Serve with whipped cream. Yields 6-8 servings.

Grandmother's Apple Pie

1 (9-inch) pie shell, partially cooked and cooled

Filling:

5-6 McIntosh or Granny Smith apples, peeled, cored and sliced	**¹/₈ teaspoon nutmeg**
²/₃ cup sugar	**¹/₈ teaspoon salt**
2 tablespoons all-purpose flour	**2 tablespoons lemon juice**
¹/₂ teaspoon cinnamon	**1 tablespoon water**

Topping:

1 cup all-purpose flour	**¹/₂ cup cold butter, cubed**
¹/₂ cup sugar	**¹/₄ cup shredded sharp Cheddar cheese**
¹/₈ teaspoon salt	**¹/₈ teaspoon cinnamon**

Preheat oven to 400 degrees. In large bowl combine apples and remaining filling ingredients, tossing gently to coat apples, and set aside. In small bowl combine flour, sugar and salt. Cut butter into flour mixture with pastry blender or fork until crumbly. Add cheese and cinnamon, tossing lightly. Transfer apple mixture to pie shell. Sprinkle topping over apples. Set pie pan on top of aluminum foil to catch juices and bake for 45 minutes. Yields 6-8 servings.

Pumpkin Cake

Butter
Sugar
1   package (18 ounce)
    yellow cake mix
2   teaspoons cinnamon

1   teaspoon allspice
1/3 cup cooking oil
3   eggs
1/2 cup sugar
1   can (16 ounce) pumpkin

Preheat oven to 350 degrees. Generously butter and sugar Bundt pan. In large mixing bowl combine cake mix and remaining ingredients, beating with electric mixer on medium speed 2 minutes. Bake for 40 to 45 minutes. Cool in pan 10 minutes; invert on rack and cool completely before slicing. Yields 10-12 servings.

Cinnamon-Apple Cake

1 3/4 cups sugar, divided
1   package (8 ounce)
    cream cheese, softened
1/2 cup butter, softened
1   teaspoon vanilla extract
2   eggs

1 1/2 cups all-purpose flour
1 1/2 teaspoons baking powder
1/4 teaspoon salt
2   teaspoons cinnamon
3 1/4 cups chopped and peeled apples

note...
Cake may also be prepared in a 9-inch springform pan. Reduce baking time by 5 minutes.

Preheat oven to 350 degrees. In large mixing bowl beat 1 1/2 cups sugar, cream cheese, butter, and vanilla with electric mixer at medium speed until well blended (about 4 minutes). Add one egg at a time, beating well after each addition; set aside. Lightly spoon flour into dry measuring cups; level with knife. Combine flour, baking powder and salt. Add flour mixture to creamed mixture, beating at low speed until blended, and set aside. In small bowl combine remaining 1/4 cup sugar and cinnamon. Combine 2 tablespoons cinnamon mixture and apples in medium bowl, tossing well to coat; fold into batter. Pour batter into prepared 8-inch springform pan and sprinkle with remaining cinnamon mixture. Bake at 350 degrees for 1 hour, 15 minutes or until cake pulls away from sides of pan. Cool cake completely on wire rack; cut, using a serrated knife. Yields 12 servings.

Fresh Pear Cake

4 cups cored,
   peeled and chopped pears
2 cups sugar
2 eggs, beaten
2/3 cup cooking oil
1 cup chopped nuts

3 cups all-purpose flour
1 teaspoon salt
1½ teaspoons baking soda
1 teaspoon nutmeg
1 teaspoon cinnamon
½ teaspoon ground cloves

Preheat oven to 325 degrees. Combine pears and sugar, tossing well to coat, and let stand 1 hour. Add eggs, oil and nuts to pears. Sift together flour and remaining ingredients; add to pear mixture, stirring until well blended. Pour into greased and floured Bundt pan or 10-inch tube pan. Bake for 1 hour, 10 minutes. Remove from oven and cool 10 minutes before removing from pan. Remove from pan and cool on wire rack. Yields 10-12 servings.

Decadent Chocolate Cake

1 cup butter, softened
1½ cups sugar
4 eggs
½ teaspoon baking soda
1 cup buttermilk
2½ cups all-purpose flour
1½ cups semi-sweet
   chocolate chips, divided

2 bars (4 ounce) sweet baking chocolate,
   melted and cooled
2 teaspoons vanilla
½ cup chocolate syrup
4 ounces white chocolate, chopped
2 tablespoons, plus 2 teaspoons shortening

Preheat oven to 300 degrees. Cream butter and sugar, beating well with electric mixer at medium speed. Add eggs one at a time and set aside. Dissolve baking soda in buttermilk and stir well. Add to butter mixture, alternating with flour, beginning and ending with flour. Add 1 cup chocolate chips, melted chocolate, vanilla and chocolate syrup. Stir until well blended. Pour into greased and floured Bundt pan. Bake for 1 hour, 25 to 35 minutes. Check cake after 1 hour for doneness. Cake is done when it springs back to touch and starts to pull away from sides at top of cake. Invert immediately and let cool. Combine and melt white chocolate with 2 tablespoons shortening in double boiler or in microwave. Drizzle over cake. Melt remaining chocolate chips with 2 teaspoons shortening and drizzle over white chocolate. Yields 10-12 servings.

Oatmeal Cake

1½ cups boiling water
1 cup quick-cooking oats
½ cup butter, softened
1 cup sugar
1 cup brown sugar
2 eggs

1⅓ cups all-purpose flour
1 teaspoon baking soda
½ teaspoon baking powder
½ teaspoon salt
½ teaspoon cinnamon

Icing:

¼ cup butter
½ cup brown sugar
¼ cup evaporated milk

1 teaspoon vanilla
1 cup flaked coconut
½ cup chopped pecans

Preheat oven to 325 degrees. Grease and flour a 9x13-inch glass baking dish. Combine water and oatmeal; cover with aluminum foil and set aside. In large bowl cream butter and sugars with electric mixer until fluffy. Add eggs to creamed mixture. Sift together flour and next 4 ingredients. Add sifted mixture to creamed mixture, combining well. Add oatmeal, mix well and pour into pan. Bake at 325 degrees for 45 to 50 minutes or until cake tester inserted in center comes out clean. To prepare icing, combine butter, sugar and evaporated milk in small saucepan. Cook until sugar dissolves. Add vanilla, coconut, and pecans. Spread on hot cake and run under broiler a few minutes if desired. Icing may be doubled for a richer topping. Yields 12 servings.

note...

Do not use instant oatmeal as a substitute for quick-cooking oats.

White Chocolate Cake with Coconut or Praline Topping

Cake:

4	ounces white chocolate	1	teaspoon vanilla
1/2	cup boiling water	2 1/2	cups sifted cake flour
1	cup butter, softened	1/2	teaspoon salt
2	cups sugar	1	teaspoon baking soda
4	eggs, separated, at room temperature	1	cup buttermilk, at room temperature

Custard:

3 eggs, well beaten
1/2 cup sugar
1 cup milk, scalded in double boiler

Icing:

1	package (8 ounce) cream cheese, softened	1	box (16 ounce) confectioners' sugar
1/2	cup butter, softened	1	teaspoon vanilla
		4	ounces flaked coconut

Praline Sauce:

2	cups brown sugar	1/2	cup light cream
1/2	cup butter, softened	1	cup pecans
1	egg, beaten		

note...

To line cake pans, cut 3 8-inch circles of wax paper or greased parchment paper. Line the bottom of each cake pan.

Preheat oven to 350 degrees. Grease, flour and line 3 (8-inch) cake pans. In double boiler melt white chocolate in 1/2 cup boiling water, then cool. In large mixing bowl cream butter and sugar until fluffy. Add egg yolks one at a time, beating after each addition. Stir in melted chocolate and vanilla. In small bowl sift flour, salt and baking soda together. Add, alternating with buttermilk, to creamed mixture. Beat after each addition until smooth, being careful not to over beat. In a clean mixing bowl, stiffly beat egg whites and fold into batter. Pour into prepared cake pans. Bake for 30 to 40 minutes. To prepare custard, slowly add eggs and sugar to hot milk and cook until custard coats spoon. Cool, then spread between cooled cake layers. To prepare icing, cream together cream cheese, butter, confectioners' sugar and vanilla until fluffy. Frost top and sides of cake. Cover with coconut and/or Praline Sauce. To prepare Praline Sauce, combine sugar, butter, egg and cream in double boiler. Cook until thickened. Fold in pecans and cool. Drizzle over top of frosted cake. Yields 10 servings.

Cream Cheese Pound Cake

1 **package (8 ounce) cream cheese, softened**
1½ **cups butter**
3 **cups sugar**
3 **cups all-purpose flour**
6 **eggs**
3 **teaspoons vanilla**
3 **teaspoons lemon or almond extract**

Preheat oven to 325 degrees. In large bowl cream cheese and butter together with electric mixer at medium speed. Add sugar and mix well. Add eggs and flour alternately, beginning and ending with flour. Continue to beat, adding vanilla and lemon or almond extract. Pour batter into greased and floured tube pan and bake for 1 hour, 30 minutes. Remove cake from oven and cool in pan; cover with baking sheet to retain moisture while cake cools. Yields 10-12 servings.

Chocolate Chip Pound Cake

1 **package (18 ounce) yellow cake mix**
1 **package (3 ounce) chocolate instant pudding and pie mix**
½ **cup sugar**
¾ **cup cooking oil**
¾ **cup water**
4 **eggs**
1 **carton (8 ounce) sour cream**
1 **package (6 ounce) chocolate chips**
Confectioners' sugar

Preheat oven to 350 degrees. In large bowl combine cake mix, instant pudding and sugar, stirring with wooden spoon. Add oil, water and eggs, mixing well. Add sour cream and chocolate chips. Pour into greased and floured tube pan. Bake for 1 hour. Cool in pan at least 1 hour. Invert onto plate; dust with confectioners' sugar. Yields 10-12 servings.

note...
Cake may be prepared the night before and plated the following morning.

White Chocolate Mousse with Raspberry Sauce

12 ounces white chocolate
3/4 cup unsalted butter
10 eggs, separated, at room temperature
1 cup granulated sugar
2 packages (1/4 ounce) unflavored gelatin
2 tablespoons cold water
2 tablespoons hot water
1 cup heavy cream

Cut chocolate into small pieces. Melt chocolate in double boiler over hot water, being careful not to boil. In small saucepan melt butter and keep warm. Pour melted chocolate into small mixing bowl, whipping slowly until smooth. While chocolate is still warm, beat in warm butter and egg yolks. Work quickly so mixture stays warm. Mixture will separate, so continue beating until smooth and shiny and set aside. Whip egg whites until stiff. Slowly beat in sugar. Whip until very stiff and sugar dissolves. Fold into chocolate mixture. Chill 1 hour. Dissolve gelatin in cold water and set aside 10 minutes. Add hot water and stir over double boiler until clear and dissolved. Whip into chocolate mixture. Whip cream until stiff and fold into mousse mixture. Pour into individual serving dishes and chill 4 to 5 hours. Top with Raspberry Sauce. Yields 8-10 servings.

Raspberry Sauce:
2 packages (10 ounce) frozen raspberries, at room temperature
1/4-1/2 cup sugar
2 tablespoons raspberry liqueur

Press raspberries through mesh strainer using the back of a large spoon. Discard seeds and add sugar and liqueur to remaining pulp, mixing well. Sauce may be kept in refrigerator up to 2 weeks.

Bread Pudding with Lemon Sauce or Irish Whiskey Sauce

note...
Recipe may be doubled.

¼ **cup butter**	½ **cup raisins**
6 **bread slices**	¼ **teaspoon salt**
1 **cup firmly packed**	2 **eggs, lightly beaten**
dark brown sugar	2½ **cups milk, scalded**

Preheat oven to 325 degrees. Butter bread generously; dice bread and place into 1½-quart shallow baking dish. Sprinkle with sugar and raisins. Combine salt and eggs; gradually beat in milk and pour mixture over bread. Bake for 30 minutes or until set. Cut into 6 individual servings and top with sauce of choice. Yields 6 servings.

Lemon Sauce:

½ **cup sugar**	2 **tablespoons butter**
⅛ **teaspoon salt**	**Juice of 1 lemon**
2 **tablespoons cornstarch**	1 **teaspoon lemon zest**
1 **cup boiling water**	

In saucepan mix sugar, salt, and cornstarch. Gradually stir in boiling water. Cook, stirring constantly, until thickened. Remove from heat. Stir in butter, lemon juice and lemon zest. Serve warm over Bread Pudding. Yields 1¾ cups.

Irish Whiskey Sauce:

6 **egg yolks**
½ **cup sugar**
1 **cup milk**
Vanilla to taste
2 **ounces Irish Whiskey**

In mixing bowl whisk egg yolks with sugar until light and lemon colored. In separate saucepan scald milk; gradually pour into egg mixture while whisking constantly. Add vanilla and place over double boiler, whisking until sauce thickens. Remove from heat and add Irish Whiskey. Serve warm over Bread Pudding.

Macaroon Soufflé
with Hot Strawberry Sauce

note...

Place a hot moist tea towel around the bottom of the mold for 1 minute to loosen the soufflé if it is difficult to remove when inverted.

1   pint vanilla ice cream, softened slightly
2   macaroons, crumbled
4   teaspoons orange juice or Grand Marnier
1/2   cup heavy cream
1-2 tablespoons chopped, toasted almonds
1-2 teaspoons confectioners' sugar
Strawberries, for garnish

Combine ice cream, crumbled macaroons and orange juice or Grand Marnier in large bowl and set aside. Whip heavy cream until thickened and glossy. Fold into ice cream mixture. Spoon into 3-cup mold. Sprinkle surface lightly with almonds and confectioners' sugar. Cover with plastic wrap; freeze until firm. Invert onto serving dish and surround with whole strawberries. Pour Hot Strawberry Sauce over frozen soufflé slice and serve immediately. Yields 4-6 servings.

Hot Strawberry Sauce:
1   package (10 ounce) frozen sliced strawberries, thawed
Sugar to taste
4   teaspoons orange juice or Grand Marnier

In small saucepan combine strawberries, sugar, and orange juice or Grand Marnier. Simmer until berries are warmed through.

Pavlova

Parchment paper
4 egg whites,
   at room temperature
Pinch of salt
1 cup, less 2 tablespoons
   sugar
1/2 teaspoon vanilla

1 teaspoon white wine vinegar
1 tablespoon cornstarch
1/2 cup heavy cream
2 cups chopped seasonal
   fruit and berries combined
2 tablespoons confectioners' sugar
1/4 teaspoon vanilla

Preheat oven to 400 degrees. Beat egg whites and salt with electric mixer 5 to 6 minutes on high speed. Add sugar, vanilla and vinegar, beating until stiff. Fold in cornstarch. Place parchment paper on baking sheet. Draw an eight-inch circle. Fill in circle with meringue and build up sides with back of spoon, creating a bowl effect. Transfer to oven and immediately reduce heat to 250 degrees. Bake 1 hour, 30 minutes. Do not open oven door. Cool and chill. Whip heavy cream with confectioners' sugar and vanilla until thick and fluffy. Spoon into meringue bowl. Top with fresh fruit and serve within 1 hour. Yields 6 servings.

note...

- *Pavlova may be doubled to serve 12. Make circle 11 inches in diameter but bake same amount of time.*

- *For individual servings, make circles 3 inches in diameter but bake same amount of time.*

Homemade Peach Cobbler

1/2 cup butter
3/4 cup all-purpose flour
1/8 teaspoon salt
2 teaspoons baking powder
13/4 cups sugar, divided
3/4 cup milk
3 cups sliced peaches

Place butter in bottom of an 8x8-inch baking pan and place in oven while preheating to 350 degrees. Combine flour, salt, baking powder and 1 1/2 cups sugar in large bowl. Slowly add milk, stirring constantly. Pour batter over melted butter in baking pan. Arrange peaches on top of batter, being careful not to stir. Sprinkle with remaining 1/4 cup sugar. Place pan on baking sheet and bake for 1 hour. Yields 8-10 servings.

Delicious Apple Crisp

Filling:

10-12 cups peeled, cored and chunked apples (Granny Smith)

Juice of 2 oranges

3-4	tablespoons lemon juice
3/4	cup sugar
3-4	tablespoons instant tapioca
1 1/2	teaspoons cinnamon
1	teaspoon nutmeg
1/2	teaspoon salt
1 1/2	cups raisins, optional
1/4	cup water

Pie crust for 13x9x2-inch Pyrex pan, frozen or homemade

Vanilla ice cream

Crisp:

1/2	cup all-purpose flour
1/2	cup nonfat dry milk powder
1	cup sugar
1/2	teaspoon salt
1/2	cup butter

Preheat oven to 375 degrees. In large bowl toss apples with remaining filling ingredients. Line bottom and sides of 13x9x2-inch glass casserole dish with pie crust. In large bowl mix flour and next 4 ingredients with pastry blender or fork until crumbly. Pour apples over pie crust and cover evenly with topping. Bake for 50 minutes to 1 hour. Serve warm with vanilla ice cream. Yields 10 servings.

Blueberry Buckle

3   cups, plus 2 tablespoons
     sifted all-purpose flour
3   teaspoons baking powder
3/4   teaspoon salt
6   tablespoons unsalted butter,
     softened
1 1/4 cups sugar

1   extra large egg
3/4   cup milk
1 1/2 pints blueberries
1   cup heavy cream
1/4   cup confectioners' sugar
1/2   teaspoon vanilla
Rum

Preheat oven to 375 degrees. Sift together 3 cups flour, baking powder, and salt; set aside. Cream butter and sugar until fluffy (about 3 minutes). Beat in egg. Add flour mixture in 3 parts, alternating with milk. Toss berries with remaining flour (in order to separate and scatter evenly throughout batter) and fold in. Pour batter into greased 8-inch springform pan. Prepare topping. Sprinkle topping over batter, spreading evenly. Bake 1 hour. Test for doneness by inserting a cake tester. If not clean, bake additional 5 to 10 minutes. Cool, then run a knife around edges and remove from pan. Whip heavy cream until almost stiff. Add confectioners' sugar and vanilla. Continue to whip until thick and fluffy. Serve with whipped cream generously spiked with rum. Yields 6-8 servings.

Topping:

1/4   cup unsalted butter, softened
1/2   cup sugar

1/3   cup sifted all-purpose flour
1/2   teaspoon cinnamon

In large bowl combine all ingredients with a fork until crumbly.

Banana Rum Salsa

2   ripe bananas
2   tablespoons sugar
2   tablespoons rum
2   teaspoons butter, melted

1/2   teaspoon cinnamon
1/2   teaspoon vanilla
Vanilla ice cream

Cut bananas lengthwise and place on broiler rack. Sprinkle with sugar and broil about 6 minutes. Chop up bananas, add remaining ingredients and serve warm over vanilla ice cream. Yields 2-4 servings.

Kahlúa Freeze

note...

This dessert is also beautifully presented when prepared in a 10-inch springform pan and cut into wedges.

¼   **cup butter**

1   **package (8 ounce) chocolate wafer cookies, crumbled**

½   **gallon coffee ice cream or frozen yogurt, softened**

¼   **cup Kahlúa or other coffee liqueur**

Chocolate Fudge Sauce

1   **pint heavy cream**

1   **tablespoon crème de cacao or amaretto**

½   **cup sliced almonds, toasted lightly**

¼   **cup confectioners' sugar**

Melt butter in 9x13-inch baking pan. Spread crumbled cookies on bottom of pan, pressing to absorb butter. Spread ice cream over cookies. Pour Kahlúa over top and spread over ice cream. Freeze several hours. Remove from freezer and spread Chocolate Fudge Sauce over ice cream. Return to freezer. Whip heavy cream with confectioners' sugar and stir in crème de cacao or amaretto. Spread over Chocolate Fudge Sauce and top with toasted almonds. Place in freezer and remove dessert 5-10 minutes before serving. Cut into squares and drizzle with additional Kahlúa if desired. Yields 10-12 servings.

Chocolate Fudge Sauce:

3   **ounces bittersweet baking chocolate**

1   **ounce milk chocolate**

4   **tablespoons butter**

½   **cup sugar**

¼   **cup water**

1   **tablespoon light corn syrup**

¼   **cup sweetened condensed milk**

Melt chocolates and butter in double boiler; remove from heat and set aside. Combine sugar, water and corn syrup in small saucepan. Boil until sugar dissolves, stirring constantly. Reduce heat and simmer 5 minutes; remove from heat. Add sugar mixture and condensed milk to chocolate mixture. Beat until smooth and light.

Chocolate Oatmeal Squares

14 ounces caramel squares
1/3 cup milk
2 cups all-purpose flour
2 cups quick-cooking oats
1¼ cups brown sugar, packed

1 teaspoon baking soda
1 egg, beaten
1 cup butter, melted
1 cup mini-chocolate chips

Preheat oven to 350 degrees. Place the caramel squares and milk in saucepan and melt over low heat, being careful not to burn. In medium bowl mix together flour and next 5 ingredients. Press half of flour mixture into bottom of well greased 9x13-inch baking pan. Bake for 10 minutes. Evenly sprinkle chocolate chips and drizzle caramel over bottom layer. Sprinkle with remaining flour mixture. Return to oven for additional 20 minutes. Cool and cut into bars. Yields 10 servings.

Cranberry Squares

1½ cups sugar
2 large eggs
3/4 cup unsalted butter,
    melted and cooled slightly
1 teaspoon almond extract

1½ cups all-purpose flour
1½ cups fresh or frozen
    cranberries (about 8 ounces)
½ cup chopped pecans
1 tablespoon butter

Preheat oven to 350 degrees. Beat sugar and eggs in large bowl with electric mixer until slightly thickened (about 2 minutes). Beat in melted butter and almond extract. Add flour, stirring until well blended. Fold in cranberries and pecans. Pour batter into buttered 9x9-inch baking pan. Bake for 1 hour or until cake tester inserted into center comes out clean. Transfer to wire rack and cool completely. Cut into squares and serve. Yields 8-10 servings.

Wonderful Brownies

½ cup butter
1   cup sugar
4   eggs
1   can (16 ounce) chocolate syrup
1   cup plus 1 tablespoon all-purpose flour

Preheat oven to 350 degrees. Combine butter, sugar and eggs in medium bowl. Add syrup and flour, mixing well. Pour batter into greased and floured 9x13-inch pan. Bake for 30 minutes. Yields 12 servings.

Icing:
6   tablespoons butter
6   tablespoons milk
1½ cups sugar
¾ cup chocolate chips

Heat butter, milk and sugar in small saucepan. Bring to a boil for 30 seconds. Do not boil longer. Remove from heat and add chocolate chips, stirring until melted. Pour over warm brownies. Set aside to cool. Icing will firm in 2 to 3 hours.

Graham Cracker Brownies

12 ounces semi-sweet
    chocolate chips
2   cups graham cracker crumbs
1-2 cups chopped pecans
½   teaspoon salt
2   teaspoons vanilla
2   cans (14 ounce) sweetened condensed milk
Butter

Preheat oven to 350 degrees. Combine chocolate chips and next 4 ingredients in large bowl and mix thoroughly. Add condensed milk, stirring until moistened. Line a 9x13-inch baking pan with heavy-duty aluminum foil extending up and over sides. Butter foil generously. Spread brownie mixture evenly in pan. Bake for 25 to 35 minutes or until brown around edges and edges begin to pull away from sides of pan. Do not overcook. Lift foil out of pan. Cool slightly and cut into squares while warm. Brownies appear soft, but will firm quickly. Yields 12 servings.

Old-Fashioned Shortbread

1   cup butter plus additional butter to prepare pan
1/2 cup sugar
2 1/2 cups all-purpose flour
Fresh fruit, optional
Whipped cream, optional

Preheat oven to 300 degrees. Blend butter and sugar in food processor. Add flour and continue blending until of even consistency. Press into buttered 11x17-inch baking pan. Bake for 30 to 35 minutes until light brown. Cool and cut into squares. Serve as a cookie or top with fresh fruit and whipped cream. Yields 2-3 dozen.

note...
This particular shortbread tends to crumble, but works fine for shortcake topped with fruit and whipped cream.

Grandmother's Best Sugar Cookies

1/2	cup butter	2	tablespoons milk
1/2	teaspoon salt	2	cups sifted all-purpose flour
1	teaspoon vanilla	1	teaspoon baking powder
1	cup sugar	1/2	teaspoon baking soda
1	egg		Nutmeg

Preheat oven to 375 degrees. In large bowl blend butter, salt, vanilla and sugar together with electric mixer at medium speed. Beat in egg and milk. Stir in flour, baking powder and baking soda, mixing well. Roll into small balls and place on greased baking sheet. Spray bottom of small drinking glass with nonstick cooking spray, then dip into sugar. Lightly press down on cookie dough to flatten. Sprinkle with nutmeg. Bake for 7 to 10 minutes, or until lightly browned. Yields about 3 dozen.

Oatmeal Drop Cookies

1/2 cup shortening, softened	1 teaspoon salt
1 1/2 cups sugar	1 teaspoon cinnamon
2 large eggs	2 cups rolled oats
6 tablespoons molasses	1/2 cup chopped nuts
1 3/4 cups sifted all-purpose flour	1 cup raisins
1 teaspoon baking soda	

Preheat oven to 350 degrees. In large bowl combine thoroughly shortening, sugar, eggs and molasses. Sift together flour, soda, salt and cinnamon. Stir in oats, nuts, and raisins. Drop by teaspoonfuls about 2 inches apart on lightly greased baking sheet. Bake for 8 to 10 minutes or until lightly browned. Cool on racks and store in tightly sealed container. Yields about 4 dozen.

Chocolate Fudge Sauce

1 package (6 ounce) semi-sweet chocolate chips
1 square unsweetened chocolate
1/3 cup butter
2 cups confectioners' sugar
2 cans (5 ounce) evaporated milk
1 teaspoon vanilla or more to taste

Place chocolates and butter in microwave safe bowl and microwave 1 1/2 minutes on medium high or until melted. Beat with whisk until smooth. Stir in remaining ingredients. Beat again until smooth. Microwave 2 1/2 to 3 minutes on medium high and stir. Microwave another 2 1/2 to 3 minutes until bubbly. Transfer to sealed container and chill. The fudge will thicken in the refrigerator. When ready to use, scoop out desired amount and microwave to warm. Refrigerate unused sauce. Yields about 3 cups.

Langestraat Brugess
by John Cook

Notes...

- *Use eggs marked "large" for the recipes in this section.*
- *Because it doesn't get hot, a wooden spoon with a long handle is the best choice for stirring foods while they cook.*

Children's Recipes

Monster Cookies 182

Powdered Sugar Cookies 182

Pecan Cookies 183

Fruity Shakes 184

Frozen Yogurt Pops 184

Fruit Jigglers 185

Apricot Oatmeal Bars. 186

Homemade Ice Cream Sandwiches 187

Chocolate Cupcake Cones 188

Colored Frosting 189

Chocolate Mousse 190

Nutty Clusters 191

Kaleidoscope Fruit Salad 192

Microwave Fudge 193

Peanut Butter Fingers. 193

note...

You may substitute peanut butter chips for 3 oz. of the chocolate chips.

Monster Cookies

½	pound butter	½	tablespoon white syrup
1½	pounds peanut butter, chunky	½	tablespoon vanilla
1	pound brown sugar	4	teaspoons baking soda
2	cups granulated sugar	10	cups quick oatmeal
6	eggs	1	pound candy-coated chocolate pieces
		6	ounces chocolate chips

Combine all ingredients, except for the chocolate chips and candy-coated chocolate pieces, mixing well. Fold in chocolate candies and chocolate chips. Drop round tablespoons of dough on a greased cookie sheet and flatten slightly. Bake at 350 degrees for 6-8 minutes. Cook completely before removing from cookie sheet. Yields about 120 cookies.

Powdered Sugar Cookies

2	sticks butter
2	cups flour
1	cup pecans or walnuts, chopped
1	teaspoon vanilla
½	cup powdered sugar

Preheat oven to 350 degrees. Combine butter, flour, nuts and vanilla in a mixing bowl. Shape dough into crescents or balls. Bake for 20 minutes. Roll in powdered sugar. Yields about 4 dozen.

Pecan Cookies

1   **cup butter, room temperature**
²/₃ **cup sugar**
Pinch of salt
1   **teaspoon vanilla extract**
2   **cups all-purpose flour**
½   **cup chopped pecans**

In a large mixing bowl, combine butter, sugar, salt and vanilla. Using an electric mixer set on medium speed, beat the mixture until it is smooth. Turn off the mixer a few times to scrape down the sides of the bowl with a rubber spatula. Add the flour and nuts. Continue mixing until the dough looks like moist pebbles, then turn off the mixer. Gently squeeze the dough together with your hands. When the dough comes together in a mass, place it on a large piece of plastic wrap. Using your hands, shape into a log 10 inches long and about 2 inches in diameter. Wrap the log in the plastic wrap and refrigerate until firm, about 3 hours. Preheat the oven to 350 degrees. Line three baking sheets with aluminum foil. Unwrap the dough and place on a cutting board. Using a knife, cut the log into slices ¼ inch thick. Arrange the slices about 1 inch apart on the foil-lined baking sheets. Place 1 baking sheet in the oven and bake the cookies until their edges are golden brown, 14 to 16 minutes. Using oven mitts, remove the baking sheet from the oven and set on a rack to cool completely. Repeat with the second and then third baking sheets. Lift the cooled cookies off the baking sheets with your fingers. Store the cookies in an airtight container. Yields about 40 cookies.

Fruity Shakes

8 ounces vanilla yogurt
2 teaspoons sugar
6 strawberries, stems cut off
   OR 1 small ripe peach, pit removed and cut into chunks
1 cup blueberries
Ice cubes (optional)

Put yogurt and sugar in an electric blender. Add your choice of fruit. Place the lid securely on the blender. Make sure it's on tight! Hold down the lid with your hand (so the spinning liquid doesn't force it off) and turn the blender on high speed. Blend until thick and smooth. If you want your shake frostier, fill 1 or 2 glass(es) with ice cubes and pour the shake into the glass(es). Serve immediately. Yields 1 or 2 servings.

Frozen Yogurt Pops

1 cup strawberry yogurt
1 cup orange juice
1½ cups raspberry juice

Set 5-ounce popsicle molds or paper cups on a work surface. Spoon an equal amount of yogurt into each mold or cup and press down with a spoon to fill the bottom evenly. Cover the molds. If using cups, cover each with a square of aluminum foil, pressing it firmly around the sides. Poke a popsicle stick through each foil cover, pushing it into the middle of the yogurt. Set the molds or cups in the freezer until beginning to set, about 40 minutes. Remove the molds from the freezer. If using cups, carefully lift off the foil, but leave the sticks in place. Pour an equal amount of the orange juice into each mold or cup. Cover, return the molds or cups to the freezer, and freeze until firm, about 40 minutes. Repeat the procedure with the raspberry juice. Freeze until solid, about 4 hours or overnight. To serve, slip the pops from the molds or remove the foil and peel away the paper cups. Yields 8 pops.

Fruit Jiggles

4 cups apple juice
2 envelopes unflavored gelatin
2 cups mixed fruits such as chopped strawberries, chopped peaches,
   whole blueberries and halved seedless grapes

Have ready an 8-inch square baking dish. Make room in the refrigerator for medium size mixing bowl. Pour 1 cup of the apple juice into a small saucepan. Sprinkle the gelatin over apple juice and let stand until the gelatin plumps up, about 2 minutes. Set pan over a medium-low heat and stir with a wooden spoon until the liquid is completely clear and the gelatin is dissolved, about 6 minutes. Using a potholder, remove the pan from heat and pour the liquid into the medium-size mixing bowl. Add the remaining 3 cups apple juice and stir until blended. Set the bowl of apple juice and gelatin in the refrigerator. Chill, stirring every 5 minutes, until slightly thickened, about 1 hour. When the mixture is the consistency of unbeaten egg whites, remove it from the refrigerator and gently stir in the mixed fruit. The fruit will be suspended in the gelatin. Pour the mixture into 8-inch baking dish, cover with plastic wrap, and refrigerate until firm, about 4 hours or overnight. Spoon into serving dishes or, using an offset spatula, cut into 9 squares and serve. Yields 9 servings.

Apricot Oatmeal Bars

3/4 cup butter, cut up
2 teaspoons soft butter
for greasing foil
1 cup firmly packed
dried apricots
1½ cups old-fashioned
rolled oats

1 cup all-purpose flour
1 cup firmly packed
dark brown sugar
¼ teaspoon salt
¼ teaspoon ground cinnamon
1½ teaspoons vanilla extract

Put the 3/4-cup butter in a small saucepan and set over medium-high heat. Stir with a wooden spoon until the butter is melted, about 2 minutes. Using a potholder, remove the saucepan from the heat and set it aside to cool. Preheat the oven to 350 degrees. Line the bottom and sides of a 9-inch square baking pan with a large piece of aluminum foil (some foil hanging over the edges is fine). Lightly grease the foil with the soft butter. Using kitchen scissors, snip the apricots into about ½-inch pieces. In a medium mixing bowl, combine the rolled oats, flour, brown sugar, salt and cinnamon. Mix with a wooden spoon until well blended and no lumps of sugar remain. Add the snipped apricots, melted butter, and vanilla to the bowl. Stir until well blended. The dough will be moist and crumbly. Dump the dough into the prepared baking pan. Press the dough into the pan with your fingers. Bake until the top is golden brown, 35 to 40 minutes. Using a pair of oven mitts, remove the pan from the oven and set on a rack to cool completely. Lift the foil and oatmeal bars from the pan and place on a work surface. Using a small, sharp knife, cut the big square into 11x2x3-inch rectangles. Store in an airtight container. Yields 18 bars.

Homemade Ice-Cream Sandwiches

1	tablespoon butter, room temperature, for greasing foil	1½	cups sugar
		3	eggs
¾	cup butter (1½ sticks)	2	teaspoons vanilla extract
¾	cup unsweetened cocoa powder	1½	cups all-purpose flour
		1	quart chocolate chip ice cream, softened
			Salt for taste

note...
You can also wrap the sandwiches in plastic wrap and store them in the freezer for up to 2 weeks.

Preheat oven to 350 degrees. Line the bottom and sides of a 9x13-inch pan with aluminum foil (some foil hanging over the edges is fine). Lightly grease the foil with butter. Put the ¾ cup butter into a saucepan and set it over medium heat. Stir with a whisk just until the butter is melted. Using a potholder, remove the saucepan from the heat and add cocoa powder. Whisk until the mixture is smooth and no lumps remain. Add the sugar and continue whisking until well blended. Let the mixture cool for 2 minutes. Add the eggs and vanilla and whisk until well blended. Add the flour and salt. Using a rubber spatula, stir until the batter is blended. Scrape down the sides of the saucepan as needed. Bake for 15-20 minutes. Using the ends of the foil, lift the brownie from the pan and set it on a cutting board. Cut the brownie in half lengthwise. Carefully loosen both halves from the foil. Using the rubber spatula, spread the softened ice cream evenly over one half of the brownie into a layer about 1 inch thick. Top with the other half of the brownie and press down gently. Wrap in the foil. Freeze until hard, about 6 hours. Peel away the foil and cut into 8 to 10 sandwiches. Serve immediately. Yields 8-10 sandwiches.

Chocolate Cupcake Cones

10 flat-bottomed waffle cones

1 cup all-purpose flour

⅓ cup unsweetened
cocoa powder

1¾ teaspoons baking powder

¼ teaspoon salt

¼ cup butter, room temperature,
cut into pieces

½ cup sugar

1 egg

½ cup milk

1 teaspoon vanilla extract

1 recipe colored frosting (see page 189)

Colored sprinkles

Preheat oven to 350 degrees. Check the cones for holes or cracks and replace if necessary. Put each cone into a cup of a muffin pan. In a small mixing bowl, combine the flour, cocoa, baking powder and salt. Stir with a table fork until blended. In a medium mixing bowl, combine the butter, sugar and egg. Using an electric mixer set on medium speed, beat until the mixture is lighter in color and no lumps remain, about 2 minutes. Turn off the mixer a few times so you can scrape down the sides of the bowl with a rubber spatula. Add the milk and vanilla. Reduce the speed to low and beat until smooth, stopping to scrape down the sides of the bowl as needed. Add the flour mixture to the butter-sugar mixture all at once. Using the rubber spatula, stir gently until the batter is completely moistened and combined. Using a spoon, place even amounts of the batter, about 3 tablespoons, into each cone. Gently tap the bottom of the cone on your palm to settle the batter. Bake the cupcakes until a toothpick inserted into the center of 1 cake comes out clean, 25 to 28 minutes. Using oven mitts, remove the muffin pan from the oven and set it on a rack. Let cool completely. Using an icing spatula, spread 1 heaping tablespoon of the frosting on each cupcake. Using your fingers, sprinkle the tops with the colored sprinkles. Serve immediately or cover loosely with plastic wrap and store at room temperature for up to 1 day. Yields 10 cupcakes.

Colored Frosting

6 tablespoons butter, room temperature
1½ cups confectioners' sugar, sifted if lumpy
2 tablespoons heavy cream
¾ teaspoon vanilla extract
3 ounces unsweetened chocolate, chopped (optional)
Food coloring (optional)

Vanilla frosting:

In a medium mixing bowl, combine the butter, confectioners' sugar, cream and vanilla. Using an electric mixer set on low speed, beat until the mixture is smooth. Turn off the mixer several times so you can scrape down the sides of the bowl with a rubber spatula. Use frosting immediately.

Colored frosting:

Make vanilla frosting as directed above. Add a drop or two of food coloring to the frosting and mix until thoroughly blended. Alternatively, divide the frosting among 2 or 3 small bowls and mix a different color into each bowl. Use frosting immediately.

Chocolate frosting:

Make vanilla frosting as directed above. Fill a small saucepan half full with water. Choose a small, deep heatproof bowl that fits snugly on the saucepan. Be sure the bottom of the bowl does not touch the water. Add the chocolate to the small bowl and set the whole thing (water-filled pan and bowl) over medium heat. Heat the chocolate, stirring with a wooden spoon until it is melted, about 5 minutes. Using a potholder, remove the pan from the heat. Ask an adult to help you remove the bowl from the saucepan of water. BE CAREFUL: THE STEAM IS VERY HOT! Set the bowl aside to cool. Stir in the melted and cooled chocolate into the frosting until well blended. Use frosting immediately.
Yields 1 cup.

Chocolate Mousse

1¼ cups semisweet chocolate chips,
    OR 8 ounces semisweet chocolate, chopped
2   cups heavy cream, well chilled

Fill a small saucepan half full with water. Choose a small, deep heatproof bowl that fits snugly on the saucepan. Be sure the bottom of the bowl does not touch the water. Add the chocolate to the small bowl and set the whole thing (water-filled pan and bowl) over medium heat. Heat the chocolate, stirring often with a wooden spoon, until it is melted, about 5 minutes. During that time, the water should simmer, not boil. Adjust the heat up or down as necessary. Turn off the heat. Ask an adult to remove the bowl from the saucepan of water. Set the bowl aside to cool slightly. Pour the cream into a large mixing bowl. Using an electric mixer set on medium speed, beat the cream until slightly thickened, about 30 seconds. Add the warm chocolate to the cream. Continue beating on medium speed, scraping down the sides of the bowl with a rubber spatula, until soft peaks form, about 1 minute. To test, turn off the mixer and lift the beaters. If the cream makes soft little peaks that flop over slightly, it is ready. Spoon the mousse into serving cups or glasses. Cover with plastic wrap and refrigerate for at least 2 hours before serving. Yields 8 servings.

Nutty Clusters

1   **tablespoon soft butter for greasing baking sheets**
2   **egg whites**
½   **cup firmly packed light brown sugar**
1   **teaspoon vanilla extract**
Pinch of salt
1   **cup sliced almonds**
1   **cup chopped pecans**
1   **cup chopped walnuts**

Preheat the oven to 350 degrees. Line 2 baking sheets with aluminum foil and lightly grease with the 1 tablespoon soft butter. In a mixing bowl, combine the egg whites, brown sugar, vanilla and pinch of salt. Stir with a table fork, mashing any lumps of sugar, until the mixture is frothy and smooth. Add the almonds, pecans and walnuts. Mix with a fork until all the nuts are well coated, scraping down the sides of the bowl with a rubber spatula. Drop heaping tablespoonfuls of the nut mixture onto the prepared baking sheets, spacing them about 2 inches apart. As you work, scrape down the sides of the bowl and stir the mixture occasionally. Flatten mounds slightly. Place one baking sheet in the oven and bake until the nuts are well browned, 14 to 16 minutes. Using oven mitts, remove the baking sheet from the oven and set it on a rack to cool completely. Bake the second sheet of clusters. Using your fingers, carefully peel the cooled clusters from the foil. Store in an airtight container at room temperature for up to one week. Yields 24 clusters.

Kaleidoscope Fruit Salad

2	**ripe plums**
1	**ripe nectarine or peach**
2	**cups strawberries**
1	**cup blueberries**
1	**cup raspberries**
½	**cored, peeled pineapple (store bought)**
1	**orange**
2	**tablespoons sugar (optional)**

Rinse and dry off the plum and nectarine or peach. Carefully rinse and dry off the berries. On a cutting board, using a small, sharp knife, cut off the green stems from the strawberries. Cut the strawberries in half lengthwise and put them in a large mixing bowl. Cut each plum in half, remove the pit, and cut each half into wedges. Add to the bowl. Do the same to the nectarine or peach and add to the bowl along with the blueberries and the raspberries. Place the pineapple, flat side down, on the cutting board. Cut into 1-inch-thick slices. Cut each half circle into 4 chunks and add to the bowl. Using a sharp knife, cut the orange across the middle. Hold each half over the small bowl and squeeze. Pick out any seeds and measure ¼ cup juice. Sprinkle the fruits with the sugar, if using, and the ¼ cup juice. Gently toss the fruits with wooden spoon until well mixed. Cover the bowl with plastic wrap and refrigerate for at least 1 hour to chill well. When ready to serve, divide the fruit salad among serving bowls and spoon the juice over the top. Yields 8 servings.

Microwave Fudge

1   pound powdered sugar
1   stick margarine
⅓   cup cocoa
¼   cup evaporated milk
1 teaspoon vanilla
Nuts (optional)

In a microwave safe bowl, pour (DO NOT STIR) powdered sugar, margarine, cocoa and evaporated milk. Microwave on high for 2 minutes. Remove from microwave and add vanilla. Beat with a mixer until smooth, stir in nuts (as many as you would like), if desired. Pour into a 9x9 pan and let cool. Cut and serve. Yields 12 servings.

Peanut Butter Fingers

½   cup butter
½   cup brown sugar
1   egg
⅓   cup peanut butter
½   teaspoon baking soda

¼   teaspoon salt
½   teaspoon vanilla
½   cup sugar
1   cup flour
1   cup rolled oats

Cream butter. Gradually add sugar and mix well. Blend egg, peanut butter, baking soda, salt and vanilla, mix well. Add flour (this will be really stiff at this point). Mix in the oats. Put into a 13x9 pan and bake at 350 degrees for 20-25 minutes. Apply icing. Cut into strips or fingers. Yields about 3 dozen.

Icing:
4   tablespoons peanut butter
4-6 tablespoons milk
3   cups of powdered sugar

Mix all ingredients together until spreading consistency.

Contributors

Ann Adams
Laurie Ames
Buff Amis
Sandy Ammons
Carol Anderson
Sara King Andrews
Margaret Arrington
Marilyn H. Augur
Monica Austin
Brynn Bagot
Jill Bee
Priscilla Bell
Carolyn Bender
Reggie Beuttenmuller
Mary Lee Bicknell
Kathryne Bishop
Cordelia Boone
Leslie Box
Renita Boyd
Sherri Raihall Braun
Nancy Broudy
Brenda Brown
Jane H. Browning
Dana Lou Bunten
Christy Burr
Diane Byrd
Melanie Byrne
Joyce Campbell
Nancy Carlson
Lisa Centala
Kathleen Christodolou
Rita Clinton

Kim Clow
Amber Coben
Brenda Cockerell
Serena Cole
Julie Collier
Anne Collins
Maura Costello
Peggy Crews
Rhonda Crocker
Kathy Crow
Sandra Cude
Laura Cudihee
Betsy Cullum
Nancy Curran
Jessica Dalton
Kate Dalton
Tina Danze
Jill Dardick
Jan Daulton
Mary V. Davis
Nancy Davis
Ann Delatour
Emily Deutscher
Gretchen Devero
Natalie Devero
Richard Devero
Ryland Devero
Ann Diamond
Catherine Dickson
Lillian Dona
Dian Dorsey
Sally Douglas

Jane Dunne
Amara Durham
Rusty Duvall
Sherri Edrington
Joan Eleazer
Priscilla Elliott
Laurie Ellis
Claire Emanuelson
George Farr
Wanda Farr
Susan Farris
Jennifer Feagin
T.J. Fechtel
Leslie Ficke
Elizabeth Figari
Rose Fitzgerald
Rainey Fogiel
Cindy Freeman
Margot Gill
Leslie Golden
Toppy Goolsby
Donette Green
Mary Kay Guevel
Karen Gunter
Grace Hage
Randi Halsell
Sally Hammer
Jan Harbour
Sarah Hardin
Cindy Harding
Linda Hardison
Cathy Hare

Laura Hare
Dana Harkey
Linda Harris
Jill Hassmann
Deb Herod
Lil Herpers
Martha Hooper
Mary Louise C. Hopson
Anne Hubbard
Sue Hubbard, M.D.
Blythe Hughes
Laura Humphries
Betsy Hunt
Caroline L. Hunt
Sherry Ingels
Sue Irish
Joellen Jameson
Susan Jennings
Gayle Johansen
Sarah Johnson
Mary Kardell
Tricia Koch
Rebecca Lacour
Gigi Lancaster
Marea Lange
Betsy Lawson
DeeDee Lee
Lyn Legge
Merriellen Lehner
Lynn Lemon
Bonnie Lewis
Cindy Lindsley

Gwen Longino
Cindy Lucas
Beverly Lueckemeyer
Rebecca Lutz
Betsy Field MacKay
Roblyn Mai
Sandye P. Mailandt
Wendy Marsh
Tracy McCalmont
Janet McCarty
Janet McColloch
Kimberly McDavid
Michele McDermett
Mrs. William McGinnis
Barbara McKenzie
Amy Meindl
Tanya Mendenhall
Rebecca Merrell
Natalie Lisa Metzger
Diane Milano
Jan Miller
Mary Montgomery
Ginny Moore
Patricia Murphy
Jan Myers
Leigh Myers

Elizabeth Naftalis, M.D.
Sallie Newell
Peggy Newman
Lynn Nikaidoh
Ida Papert
Patty Parker
Teresa Parravano
Karen Peck
Meg Pontrich
Pat Prestidge
Beverly J. Pruitt
Eleanor Putman
Devin Rambie
Melinda Ramsey
Susan Ray
Amy Rea
Karen Reardon
Chris Reddin
Erin Reina
Vicky Riley
Jennifer Roan
Carol Ronchetti
Kayla Roughton
Lee Rury
Julie Sadler
Karee Sampson

Karen C. Sargent
Suzi Scherer
Kathlyn Sears
Maureen Shafer
Holly Shaw
Martha Sheeder
Bonnie Shelby
Priscilla Shellenberger
Judy Sillers
Diane Smith
Robin Arnold Smith
Kim Koonce-Smith
Debbie Snell
Marinelle Sowden
Dillard Spring
Jo Stage
Lynn Stelling
Jennifer Stephens
Jeanine Stevens
Mary Kay Story
Belinda Stuart
Venise Stuart
Jane Switzer
Natalie Taylor
Laine Thayer
Kay Theis

Carolyn Toledo
Tamareh Tuma
Kathy Vandemotter
Susan Viracola
Vermelle Votteler
Nancy Walker
Grace Walker
Dawna Hamm Walsh
Candy Ward
Becky Nelson Warren
Marilyn Weber
Kay Weeks
Trish Weigand
Mary Kay Whaley
Jean White
Joanie Williams
Susan Williams
Susan K. Wolcott
Sally Wood
Cayla Woodruff
Allison Woram
Kimberly Yamanouchi, M.D.
Lauren Zogg

The Collection, Cures for the Common Cuisine *includes both recipes originated by members of the Women's Auxiliary to Children's Medical Center of Dallas and favorite recipes taken from other sources and refined by the cookbook testing committee to meet the goal of making sophisticated cooking easy and enjoyable.*

Tributes

In loving memory of Thomas Mott Rambie.
The Mark Aldredge Family

Dallas, Texas is blessed to have Children's Medical Center!
The Ames Family

1985 Off Preston Gourmet Dinner Club Friendship, Food & Spirits!
Mr. and Mrs. Dave Anderson

In honor of all past presidents of the Women's Auxiliary.
Mrs. Martha Lou Beaird

In honor of my family; husband, William L. Berry, M.D.; son and wife, Scott & Sarah; and daughter, Heather.
Dr. Priscilla M. Berry

In memory of Grandma Blewett and Yiaya Chantilis, who could make the best pies and Greek pastries I have ever tasted.
Mrs. Stephanie Bray

With love to Sloane, Shea, Blakeley, Christopher and Will and all their friends and family.
Mrs. Sarah Castleman

Mixing love for Dallas with tremendous talent and abounding energy has long been the recipe for success for our friends, Hal and Diane Brierley. The collection of community organizations that have benefited from their tireless efforts will forever be grateful to them.
With greatest respect, Chuck and Diane Cheatham

To Krissi Holman, who called my cookies "her medicine" and whose courage and sense of humor exemplifies the patients at Children's Medical Center.
Mrs. Sandra Cude

In memory of my Grandma Hardt and Grandmother Waterhouse, both who passed on much more than their recipes.
Mrs. Jill Dardick

In honor of Elizabeth, Franklin, and Pierce Davis.
Mrs. Lee Davis

DUXIANA
Compliments of Serena & Michael Cole

GALLERIA/HINES
GALLERIA, a project of Hines

In memory of a loving mother and fantastic cook, Manon Ray Murray.
Mrs. Melissa Gioldasis

We are thankful to God for our healthy children, Hawkins and Houston Golden.
Mrs. Leslie Golden

To "Mama Hoppy," whose main ingredient has always been LOVE!
Mrs. Jayne Grimes

In honor of Tracey Dobbins for her contributions to The Ronald McDonald House of Dallas.
The Mike Hainsfurther Family

In honor of Dr. Mark Hardin, who has helped countless sick children.
Mrs. Sarah Hardin

In honor of Drs. Bryan Dickson, Amy Hogge, Patrick Leavey and Steve Megison. And in memory of Callie Curnes.
Mrs. Susan K. Holman

This cookbook is dedicated to the volunteers who helped make it possible and to every-one who appreciates good food.
Hook, Line & Sinker

Devin, you are the best part of *The Collection*. Congratulations! We love you!
Judy, Lee and Martha

In honor of Nancy Broaddus Hunt and W. Herbert Hunt, parents and inlaws. Thanks for all the years of Sunday lunches and holidays cooked up in your home. What great memories and role models you have provided for all of us. We love you.
Margaret & Douglas H. Hunt

In honor of Bebe Mills Flynn, my mom. Thanks for all the wonderful family recipes you have passed on to me, and the fun we shared making and discussing them through the years. We love you and we all love your cooking!
Margaret Flynn Hunt

In memory of Callie Curnes, my "cuz," for teaching me about friendship, strength, family, trust, faith, and love. Thank you for having been the kind of person I strive to be.
Megan Hunt

Dr. Alvis Johnson, Jr., was one of the pioneer pediatric cardiologists in Texas. He taught and practiced Pediatric Cardiology at Children's from 1952 to 1983. His dedication to helping children with heart problems was accompanied by a life long passion for Texas barbecue. Today, at 84, he is equally at home in the kitchen as he was in a medical environment. This tribute is made by his loving children and their spouses, Beverly and Tom Smith, Sarah Johnson and John May, Craig and Susan Johnson, Becca and Joe Munsch, Scott and Julie Johnson, his eight grandchildren and one granddaughter-in-law.
Dr. Alvis Johnson's Children

To my daughters, Katie and Caroline Koch: The breaking of bread together is a warm bond between families, friends and those we seek to honor. May you sit down and grow and learn and laugh in the communion of food.
Joy to you and yours, Mama (Tricia Koch)

To my husband, Patrick Lacy, who really "cooks!"
Love, Amy

Brenda and Tanya, it was a privilege to work with you on this cookbook. May the profits exceed our dreams for the patients at Children's!
DeeDee

In loving memory of our son, Connor Raymond Marlow.
Mr. and Mrs. David Marlow

To my mother, Joan Palmisano, for cooking that warms the heart.
Kimberly McDavid

To the very special women in our lives, Miss Clara, Nano, Granny Doc, Betty, Carolyn and Shirley, who all taught us the meaning of a warm home, a warm kitchen and a warm heart. We love you very much.
Michele, Don, Megan and Bonner McDermett

In loving honor of my children and their spouses, Melinda Means, Robin and Scot Skinner, Wanda and Richard Means, Jr., Amy and Jayson Bales; and my grandchildren, Jordan, Sophie, and Brock Skinner, Richard III and Elizabeth Means, and Silas Bales; and in loving memory of Richard Means, Sr.
Janie Means

To Nicole and Natalie,
May love be the main ingredient in your recipe for life.
Love, Mom and Dad
(Mr. and Mrs. Steven C. Metzger)

Love to the treasures in my life, Frank, John, Julia, Spence, Liza, Trevor and Patrick.
Mrs. Kay Miller

Loving thanks to the ER and ICU for saving Arthur's life. What a miraculous blessing!
Mr. and Mrs. Prater Monning

To Devin and Julie and to all of their dear friends who have made *The Collection* possible.
Mr. and Mrs. Lee Mott

In honor of Drs. George Branch, Debra Burns and Victoria Shinn.
Isabell and Daniel Novakov

To our mother, Connie Mott, for countless warm and delicious family memories.
Mrs. Devin Rambie

To my mom, Brownie Shytles, the best hot roll maker in the world!
With love, Priscilla Shellenberger

Thanks to my mom, Betty Scott Ewan, for being a true inspiration as a mom, cook and teacher! She is the best that there is in all three of these areas!
With love, your daughter Brenda Shute

We lovingly honor our 4-year-old son, Austin Silvera, who has Type 1 diabetes and his supportive sister, Amanda Silvera.
Mr. and Mrs. Darryl Silvera

To Zan, Andrew and Alyson, who make my efforts the food of love.
Robin Arnold Smith

In memory of our beloved daughter and best friend, Kimberly Anne Sowden.
Mr. and Mrs. Webb Sowden

To those dedicated to making life better for children.
Mrs. Venise Stuart

To my daughter, Jordan, and my husband, Scott. You have brought magic to my life.
Love, Mom (Mrs. Jane Switzer)

In honor of and tribute to Dr. Theodore Votteler, M.D.
Thank you, Spencer and Marshall Theis

Blessed Mother, no matter how tired you were, you could always make brownies.
Love, Tamareh Tuma

To my wonderful husband who takes me out to eat and my three precious children who always compliment my food.
Love, Tamareh & Mom

Children's Medical Center of Dallas is the best hospital for children in the country!
Mrs. Kay Weeks

In honor of George Farr and Dr. Claude Prestidge.
Mr. and Mrs. Richard R. Welfelt

Thanks to all my friends who have tried to transform me into a cook!
Candace Winslow

Thanks to Susan Ray for coming up with "Cures for the Common Cuisine." It is clever, catchy and creative!
Women's Auxiliary

In honor of Drs. Rob and Janet Squires with much love and appreciation.
Mary Flo and Dave Ridley

Honoring Mary Ellen Durham and Michelle Rahman. Thank you for a lifetime of nourishment, including your love, support and devotion.
Amara Durham

To David, for your commitment to Children's and to us.
We love you, Cynthia and Abigail

To DeeDee, in recognition and appreciation of the hours upon hours of effort and commitment you gave to this cookbook. From conception to realization, always cognizant that "it's all for the children." Congratulations on a job well done! We are proud of you.
With love, Jim, Casey and Michael

To Brenda Cockerell, in recognition and appreciation of your hard work and dedication in making this cookbook a reality. Your friendship with and support of

DeeDee in this, and so many other endeavors through the years, has been incredible. Whether cooking, catering, entertaining or just enjoying life, the two of you make a great team. Casey, Michael and I also want to thank you for teaching DeeDee how to cook. As I have often said, you are the best cook I know. But with your tutelage, DeeDee is now running a strong second! Congratulations on a job well done.
Love, Jim Lee

To Debbie Snell, thank you for your confidence in asking us to chair this cookbook. We hope *Cures for the Common Cuisine* exceeds all expectations.
DeeDee Lee and Brenda Cockerell

DeeDee, some of my happiest memories are of times spent in the kitchens of women I love…my grandmother, my mother, my favorite aunt and with you. For me, our work on this cookbook has been an extension of the laughter and friendship we have shared over the years in our kitchens. I hope *Cures for the Common Cuisine* communicates, especially to our children, all of the love, laughter and joy that is to be found in cooking for others.
xo, Brenda

Thank you to the following people for their support:
Mrs. Jean C. Beasley
Dr. and Mrs. Collin Bell
Mr. and Mrs. Tom Boone
Mr. and Mrs. Steve Brooks
Mrs. Nancy Carlson
Mrs. Miriam Carroll
Mr. and Mrs. Harlan Crow
Mr. and Mrs. Dewey Dalton
Mr. and Mrs. John Delatour

Mr. and Mrs. Robert Dransfield
Mr. and Mrs. James N. Francis
The Guion Gregg, III Family
Mrs. Jan Harbour
Mrs. Caroline L. Hunt
Mrs. Kate Crosland Juett
Legacy Bank of Texas
Mr. Mary Lou Mahoney
Mrs. Wendy Marsh
Mrs. Mary D. Misdom
Mr. and Mrs. Baker Montgomery
Ms. Anne-Marie Oliver
Diane & Jim Pasant
Regency Centers
Mr. and Mrs. Lou Schaufele
Mrs. John R. Sears
Mrs. Sandra Snyder
Mr. and Mrs. Sam Stuart
Tom Thumb
Mrs. John C. Tolleson
Mrs. Marilyn Toomey
Ms. Kathryn Voreis
Mrs. Donese Walker
Mr. and Mrs. James R. Wills

Index

A

Absolutely Elegant Asparagus Soup 44
All-Purpose Meat Marinade 139
Angel Biscuits 15
Angel Hair with Red Pepper-Lime Purée 146

Appetizers (also see Dips and Spreads)

    Blue Cheese Biscuit Bites 22
    Confetti Bagel Bites 36
    Crabmeat Cream Puffs 27
    Curried Cheese Wedges 23
    Easy Cheese Wafers 22
    Last Minute Spinach Balls 25
    Paw Paw's Oysters Rockefeller 120
    Shrimp and Gruyère Tart 29
    Shrimp Ceviche 27
    Shrimp Cocktail Acapulco Style 28
    Warm Blue Cheese Appetizers 22

Apples

    Apple Cheese Nut Salad 58
    Cinnamon-Apple Cake 165
    Delicious Apple Crisp 174
    Fresh Fruit with Poppy Seed Dressing 60
    Grandmother's Apple Pie 164
    Holiday Curried Butternut Soup 45
    Pork Chops Victoria 81
    Spicy Jicama Salad 62
    Sugar and Nut Glazed Brie 23

Apricots

    Apricot Oatmeal Bars 186
    Grilled Apricot Lamb Chops 83

Wild Rice, Apricot and Almond Salad 57

Artichokes

    Artichoke Chili Dip 40
    Chicken Dijonnaise 89
    Hot Crab and Artichoke Dip 28
    Italian Chicken 87
    Marinated Shrimp, Mushroom
        and Artichoke Salad 63
    Paella Salad 150
    Spinach Chicken Crêpes 84
    Spinach-Artichoke Cheesecake 24
    Super Salad 61

Asparagus

    Absolutely Elegant Asparagus Soup 44
    Cold Asparagus with Pecans 129
    Marinated Asparagus Salad 63
    Roasted Asparagus with Hot Crab Sauce 128

Avocados

    Avocado Corn Guacamole 39
    Avocado Terrine 35
    Pasilla Chicken Enchiladas 93
    Salsa Verde 39
    Shrimp Cocktail Acapulco Style 28
    Southwestern Poolside Dip 38
    Super Salad 61
    Tomato-Avocado Salsa 142

B

Baked French Toast 11
Baked Potato Soup 47

Bananas

    Banana Nut Bread 16

    Banana Rum Salsa 175

Barbecue Shrimp 116

Barbecued Lamb Chops with Plum-Mint Sauce 82

Basil Parmesan Spread 25

Beans and Peas

    Beef Chili 52

    Black-Eyed Pea Soup 48

    Cuban Rice and Black Bean Salad 58

    German Style Black-Eyed Peas 127

    Herbed Couscous with Feta 152

    J.B.'s "Must-Try" Skinny Beans 126

    Mexican Relish 143

    Paella Salad 150

    Picnic Green Beans 126

    Rice, Black Beans and Feta Salad 57

    Super Salad 61

    Texas Venison Chili 109

    Vegetable-Beef Stew 51

    Very Easy Tuscan White Bean Soup 43

    White Chicken Chili 52

Béarnaise Sauce 66

Beef (also see Veal)

    Beef Chili 52

    Beef Fillet Steaks with Mushrooms
        and Béarnaise Sauce 66

    Beef Queso Dip 37

    Beef Tenderloin Steaks with Peppercorn Sauce 70

    Beef Tenderloin with Mushrooms 68

    Italian Meat Sauce for a Crowd 148

    Lasagna Roll-Ups 146

    Party Buffet Marinated Beef Tenderloin 69

    Roast Tenderloin of Beef with Madeira Sauce 67

    Southwestern Stew 50

    Super Easy Baby Back Ribs 70

    Super Easy Beef Brisket 71

    Vegetable-Beef Stew 51

Bell Peppers

    Angel Hair with Red Pepper-Lime Purée 146

    Cream of Roasted Red Pepper Soup 42

    Fast and Easy Polenta with Roasted Vegetables 154

Best Baby Back Ribs 80

Best Vinaigrette 136

"Best-Ever" Rice 150

Black-Eyed Pea Soup 48

Blue Cheese Biscuit Bites 22

Blueberries

    Blueberry Buckle 175

    Blueberry Coffee Cake 10

    French Café Salad 55

    Fruit Jigglers 185

    Fruity Shakes 184

    Kaleidoscope Fruit Salad 192

Bordelaise Sauce 138

Bourbon Molasses Quail or Duck Breasts 104

Braised Quail with Grapes 101

Brandied Mushroom Pie 133

Bread Pudding with
    Lemon Sauce or Irish Whiskey Sauce 171

Breads

    Angel Biscuits 15

    Banana Nut Bread 16

    Chocolate Chip Zucchini Bread 18

    Cinnamon Muffins 16

    Light and Tasty Cornbread 18

    Old-Fashioned Gingerbread 17

    Potato Rolls 19

S&S Tearoom Strawberry Bread 17
Spicy Pecan Cheese Wafers 19
Breakfast Crumb Cake 10
Bristol Style Salad Dressing 54
Broccoli Strudel 130

Brunch
Baked French Toast 11
Blueberry Coffee Cake 10
Breakfast Crumb Cake 10
Delicious Egg Casserole 13
Eggs Magda 14
Ham and Grits Quiche 13
Quiche Lorraine 11
Quiche with Almonds 12
Santa Fe Soufflé 14
Sausage Cheese Biscuits 15
Sugared Bacon 14

Brussels Sprouts with Bacon, The Best 127

C

Cabbage
Spicy Cole Slaw 53
Super Simple Slaw 53
Vegetable-Beef Stew 51
Warm Cabbage with Saga Blue Cheese 64

Carolina Barbecue Doves 98

Carrots
Carrot Soufflé 135
Vegetable-Beef Stew 51

Cashew Salad Dressing 135

Casseroles
Brandied Mushroom Pie 133
Carrot Soufflé 135

Delicious Egg Casserole 13
Gruyère Potato Gratin 157
Polenta, Tomato and Pesto Casserole 153
Santa Fe Soufflé 14
Savory Sweet Potato Gratin 159
Shrimp Marsala 119
Silky Corn Casserole 133
Spinach Spoonbread 156
Thanksgiving Oysters 120
Whipped Potatoes with a Twist 158
Zucchini au Gratin 131

Caviar
Fantastic Caviar Torte 30
Party Shrimp Mold 31

Cayenne Croutons 56

Cereals and Grains
Apricot Oatmeal Bars 186
Chocolate Oatmeal Squares 177
Decadent But Delicious Cheese Grits 155
Easy Cheese Wafers 22
Ham and Grits Quiche 13
Louisiana Grits 155
Monster Cookies 182
Oatmeal Cake 167
Oatmeal Drop Cookies 180
Peanut Butter Fingers 193

Charcoaled Leg of Lamb 83

Cheese
Apple Cheese Nut Salad 58
Artichoke Chili Dip 40
Baked Potato Soup 47
Basil Parmesan Spread 25
Beef Queso Dip 37
Blue Cheese Biscuit Bites 22

Confetti Bagel Bites 36

Crabmeat Cream Puffs 27

Curried Cheese Wedges 23

Decadent But Delicious Cheese Grits 155

Delicious Egg Casserole 13

Easy Cheese Wafers 22

Fiesta Cheesecake 36

Fresh Pear and Parmesan 59

Havarti and Corn Stuffed Chili Rellenos
    with Walnut Cream Sauce 134

Herbed Couscous with Feta 152

Hot Pineapple Scallop 23

Jalapeño Cheese Dip 37

Louisiana Grits 155

Pasilla Chicken Enchiladas 93

Pasta Timbales 147

Pesto and Sun-Dried Tomato Torte 34

Provençal Goat Cheese Gratin 33

Quiche with Almonds 12

Rice, Black Beans and Feta Salad 57

Salsa Chicken Enchiladas 94

Santa Fe Soufflé 14

Sausage Cheese Biscuits 15

Shrimp and Gruyère Tart 29

Spicy Pecan Cheese Wafers 19

Summertime Tomato Blue Cheese Spread 34

Sun-Dried Tomatoes and Feta Terrine 35

Tasty Corn and Green Chili Dip 38

Warm Blue Cheese Appetizers 22

Chicken (see Poultry)

Children's Recipes

Apricot Oatmeal Bars 186

Chocolate Cupcake Cones 188

Chocolate Mousse 190

Colored Frosting 189

Frozen Yogurt Pops 184

Fruit Jigglers 185

Fruity Shakes 184

Homemade Ice Cream Sandwiches 187

Kaleidoscope Fruit Salad 192

Microwave Fudge 193

Monster Cookies 182

Nutty Clusters 191

Peanut Butter Fingers 193

Pecan Cookies 183

Powdered Sugar Cookies 182

Chili Rubbed Quail 99

Chocolate (also see Desserts)

Chocolate Chip Pound Cake 169

Chocolate Chip Zucchini Bread 18

Chocolate Cupcake Cones 188

Chocolate Fudge Sauce 176, 180

Chocolate Mousse 190

Chocolate Oatmeal Squares 177

Decadent Chocolate Cake 166

Graham Cracker Brownies 178

Homemade Ice Cream Sandwiches 187

Kahlúa Freeze 176

Microwave Fudge 193

Monster Cookies 182

Pecan Pie with Kahlúa and Chocolate Chips 163

The Best Chocolate Pie 162

White Chocolate Cake
    with Coconut or Praline Topping 168

White Chocolate Mousse with Raspberry Sauce 170

Wonderful Brownies 178

Chunky Creamy Corn Chowder 45

Cinnamon Muffins 16

Cinnamon-Apple Cake 165

Citrus Baked New Potatoes 157

Citrus Salsa 95

Clarified Butter 103

Coconut

   Oatmeal Cake 167

   White Chocolate Cake
     with Coconut or Praline Topping 168

Cold Asparagus with Pecans 129

Colored Frosting 189

Condiments and Sauces

   All-Purpose Meat Marinade 139

   Béarnaise Sauce 66

   Best Vinaigrette 136

   Bordelaise Sauce 138

   Bristol Style Salad Dressing 54

   Cashew Salad Dressing 135

   Cayenne Croutons 56

   Citrus Salsa 95

   Clarified Butter 103

   Creamy Parmesan, Basil and Pine Nut Dressing 136

   Creole Seasoning 117

   Crispy Dijon Marinade 141

   Dijon Mustard Sauce 137

   Glazed Pecan Sprinkles for Salads 54

   Honey Mustard Glaze 75

   Hot Crab Sauce 128

   Incredible Croutons 54

   Italian Tomato Sauce 29

   Knock Your Socks Off Wild Game Marinade 110

   Lemon Cilantro Sauce 77

   Lemon Herb Dressing 122

   Lime Mayonnaise 78

   Madeira Sauce 67

Mango Salsa 142

Marinade for Pork Tenderloin
   and Venison Backstrap 140

Mexican Relish 143

Mom's Buttermilk Marinade 141

Perini Ranch Steak Rub 139

Pico de Gallo 143

Plum-Mint Sauce 82

Ponzu Marinade 123

Poppy Seed Dressing 60

Port, Rosemary and Garlic Marinade 140

Raspberry Sauce 76

Red Currant Glaze 108

Rémoulade Sauce 138

Savory Sage Marinade 110

Spicy Peanut Sauce 88

Tomato Purée 132

Tomato-Avocado Salsa 142

Tried and True Pesto 137

Walnut Cream Sauce 134

Confetti Bagel Bites 36

Corn

   Avocado Corn Guacamole 39

   Chunky Creamy Corn Chowder 45

   Corn-Potato Pancakes 156

   Creamy Poblano Chicken with Cornbread Waffles 92

   Fresh Corn and Crab Bisque 47

   Havarti and Corn Stuffed Chili Rellenos
     with Walnut Cream Sauce 134

   J.B.'s "Must-Try" Skinny Beans 126

   Mexican Relish 143

   Roasted Lobster-Corn Chowder 46

   Silky Corn Casserole 133

   Southwestern Poolside Dip 38

   Tasty Corn and Green Chili Dip 38

Texas Caesar Salad with Cayenne Croutons 56
Vegetable-Beef Stew 51

Crabmeat Cream Puffs 27
Crabmeat Remick 112
Cranberry Squares 177
Crawfish Tortellini 114
Cream Cheese Pound Cake 169
Cream of Roasted Red Pepper Soup 42
Creamy Parmesan, Basil and Pine Nut Dressing 136
Creamy Poblano Chicken with Cornbread Waffles 92
Creole Seasoning.. 117
Crispy Dijon Marinade 141
Crocked Ducks 105
Cuban Rice and Black Bean Salad 58
Cumin Rice 151
Curried Cheese Wedges 23
Curried Shrimp Dip 31
Curry Chicken with Tomatoes and Raisins 90

D

Decadent But Delicious Cheese Grits 155
Decadent Chocolate Cake 166
Delicious Apple Crisp 174
Delicious Egg Casserole 13

Desserts
Cakes
Chocolate Chip Pound Cake 169
Chocolate Cupcake Cones 188
Cinnamon-Apple Cake 165
Cream Cheese Pound Cake 169
Decadent Chocolate Cake 166
Fresh Pear Cake 166
Oatmeal Cake 167
Pumpkin Cake 165

White Chocolate Cake
with Coconut or Praline Topping 168
Candies
Microwave Fudge 193
Nutty Clusters 191
Peanut Butter Fingers 193
Cookies and Bars
Apricot Oatmeal Bars 186
Chocolate Oatmeal Squares 177
Cranberry Squares 177
Graham Cracker Brownies 178
Grandmother's Best Sugar Cookies 179
Monster Cookies 182
Oatmeal Drop Cookies 180
Old-Fashioned Shortbread 179
Pecan Cookies 183
Powdered Sugar Cookies 182
Wonderful Brownies 178
Dessert Sauces
Banana Rum Salsa 175
Chocolate Fudge Sauce 176, 180
Hot Strawberry Sauce 172
Irish Whiskey Sauce 171
Lemon Sauce 171
Praline Topping 168
Raspberry Sauce 170
Pies
Grandmother's Apple Pie 164
Meringue 162
Pecan Pie with Kahlúa and Chocolate Chips 163
Praline Pumpkin Pie 163
The Best Chocolate Pie 162
Puddings and Desserts
Banana Rum Salsa 175
Blueberry Buckle 175

Bread Pudding with Lemon Sauce
   or Irish Whiskey Sauce 171
Chocolate Mousse 190
Colored Frosting 189
Delicious Apple Crisp 174
Frozen Yogurt Pops 184
Fruit Jigglers 185
Fruity Shakes 184
Homemade Ice Cream Sandwiches 187
Homemade Peach Cobbler 173
Kahlúa Freeze 176
Macaroon Soufflé with Hot Strawberry Sauce 172
Pavlova 173
White Chocolate Mousse
   with Raspberry Sauce 170

Dijon Mustard Sauce 137
Dill Cherry Tomatoes 131

Dips and Spreads
Artichoke Chili Dip 40
Avocado Corn Guacamole 39
Avocado Terrine 35
Basil Parmesan Spread 25
Beef Queso Dip 37
Curried Shrimp Dip 31
Easy and Delicious Crab Mold 32
Fantastic Caviar Torte 30
Fiesta Cheesecake 36
Hot Crab and Artichoke Dip 28
Hot Pineapple Scallop 23
Jalapeño Cheese Dip 37
Jumbo Lump Crabmeat Dip 26
Party Salmon Mousse 26
Party Shrimp Mold 31
Pesto and Sun-Dried Tomato Torte 34
Provençal Goat Cheese Gratin 33

Salsa Verde 39
Southwestern Poolside Dip 38
Spinach-Artichoke Cheesecake 24
Sugar and Nut Glazed Brie 23
Summertime Tomato Blue Cheese Spread 34
Sun-Dried Tomatoes and Feta Terrine 35
Tasty Corn and Green Chili Dip 38

E
Eastern North Carolina Pork Barbecue 79
Easy and Delicious Crab Mold 32
Easy But Elegant Salmon en Papillote 123
Easy Cheese Wafers 22
Easy Hawaiian Chicken 90
Eggs Magda 14

F
Fantastic Caviar Torte 30
Fast and Easy Polenta with Roasted Vegetables 154
Favorite Mustard Marinated Shrimp 119
Fiesta Cheesecake 36

Fish
Easy But Elegant Salmon en Papillote 123
Glazed Grilled Salmon Fillet 121
Grilled Ponzu Marinated Salmon 123
Grilled Salmon and Vegetable Salad 122
Party Salmon Mousse 26
Pesto and Sun-Dried Tomato Torte 34
Pine Nut Crusted Snapper 124
Sautéed Salmon with Spinach 121

French Bistro Grilled Chicken 91
French Café Salad 55
Fresh Corn and Crab Bisque 47
Fresh Fruit with Poppy Seed Dressing 60

Fresh Pear and Parmesan Salad 59

Fresh Pear Cake 166

Frozen Yogurt Pops 184

Fruit Jigglers 185

Fruits (see individual listings)

Fruity Shakes 184

G

Game

Bourbon Molasses Quail or Duck Breasts 104

Braised Quail with Grapes 101

Carolina Barbecue Doves 98

Chili Rubbed Quail 99

Crocked Ducks 105

Grilled Quail 102

Grilled Venison Tenderloin
  with Red Currant Glaze 108

Hunter's Duck Ragu with Pappardelle 105

Indian-Spiced Squab 99

Knock Your Socks Off Wild Game Marinade 110

Peking Spiced Duck 106

Peppered Duck Breasts 106

Rabbit Cacciatore 107

Raspberry Glazed Quail 101

Roast Quail with Hazelnuts and Port 103

Rosemary Fried Quail 102

Savory Northern Italian Quail with Polenta 100

Spicy Dove Bites 98

Texas Venison Chili 109

Venison Backstrap with Savory Sage Marinade 110

Game Day Turkey Tailgate Sandwich 96

Garlic Sour Cream Chicken 87

German Style Black-Eyed Peas 127

Glazed Cornish Hens with Savory Stuffing 96

Glazed Grilled Salmon Fillet 121

Glazed Pecan Sprinkles for Salads 54

Graham Cracker Brownies 178

Grandmother's Apple Pie 164

Grandmother's Best Sugar Cookies 179

Grapefruits

Citrus Salsa 95

Tequila Chicken with Citrus Salsa 95

Grapes

Braised Quail with Grapes 101

Fresh Fruit with Poppy Seed Dressing 60

Fruit Jigglers 185

Grilling Recipes

Barbecued Lamb Chops with Plum-Mint Sauce 82

Beef Tenderloin Steaks with Peppercorn Sauce 70

Beef Tenderloin with Mushrooms 68

Charcoaled Leg of Lamb 83

Chicken with Spicy Peanut Sauce 88

Chili Rubbed Quail 99

French Bistro Grilled Chicken 91

Glazed Grilled Salmon Fillet 121

Grilled Apricot Lamb Chops 83

Grilled Honey Glazed Pork Tenderloin 75

Grilled Ponzu Marinated Salmon 123

Grilled Quail 102

Grilled Salmon and Vegetable Salad 122

Grilled Venison Tenderloin with Red Currant Glaze 108

Honey-Sage Pork Tenderloin 77

Pork Tenderloin with Raspberry Sauce 76

Shellfish Skewers with Asian Dipping Sauce 114

Shrimp and Jalapeño Brochettes 118

Super Easy Baby Back Ribs 70

Tequila Chicken with Citrus Salsa 95

Venison Backstrap with Savory Sage Marinade 110

Gruyère Potato Gratin 157

H

Ham and Grits Quiche 13
Havarti and Corn Stuffed Chili Rellenos
   with Walnut Cream Sauce 134
Herb Roasted Chicken Breasts 85
Herbed Couscous with Feta 152
Herbed Wild Rice with Toasted Pine Nuts 152
Holiday Curried Butternut Soup 45
Holiday Sweet Potatoes 160
Homemade Ice Cream Sandwiches 187
Homemade Peach Cobbler 173

Honey
   Chicken with Spicy Peanut Sauce 88
   Glazed Cornish Hens with Savory Stuffing 96
   Glazed Grilled Salmon Fillet 121
   Grilled Honey Glazed Pork Tenderloin 75
   Honey Mustard Glaze 75
   Honey-Sage Pork Tenderloin 77
   Spicy Family Night Meatloaf 73
Hot Crab and Artichoke Dip 28
Hot Crab Sauce 128
Hot Pineapple Scallop 23
Hot Strawberry Sauce 172
Hunter's Duck Ragu with Pappardelle 105

I

Incredible Croutons 54
Indian-Spiced Squab 99
Irish Whiskey Sauce 171
Italian Chicken 87
Italian Meat Sauce for a Crowd 148
Italian Tomato Sauce 29

J

J.B.'s "Must-Try" Skinny Beans 126
Jalapeño Cheese Dip 37
Jalapeño-Potato Soup 48
Jicama Salad, Spicy 62
Jumbo Lump Crabmeat Dip 26

K

Kahlúa Freeze 176
Kaleidoscope Fruit Salad 192
Knock Your Socks Off Wild Game Marinade 110

L

Lamb
   Barbecued Lamb Chops with Plum-Mint Sauce 82
   Charcoaled Leg of Lamb 83
   Grilled Apricot Lamb Chops 83
Lasagna Roll-Ups 146
Last Minute Spinach Balls 25
Lemon Cilantro Sauce 77
Lemon Herb Dressing 122
Lemon Sauce 171
Light and Tasty Cornbread 18
Lime Mayonnaise 78
Louisiana Grits 155
Louisiana Seafood Gumbo 115

M

Macaroon Soufflé with Hot Strawberry Sauce 172
Madeira Sauce 67
Mango Salsa 142
Marinade for Pork Tenderloin
   and Venison Backstrap 140

Marinated Asparagus Salad 63

Marinated Shrimp, Mushroom and Artichoke Salad 63

Mediterranean Chicken 91

Meringue 162

Mexican Relish 143

Microwave Fudge 193

Mom's Buttermilk Marinade 141

Monster Cookies 182

Mushrooms

    Beef Fillet Steaks with Mushrooms
      and Béarnaise Sauce 66

    Beef Tenderloin with Mushrooms 68

    Brandied Mushroom Pie 133

    Chicken Breasts
      with Garlic Balsamic Vinegar Sauce 86

    Chicken in Roquefort Sauce 89

    Italian Chicken 87

    Marinated Shrimp, Mushroom
      and Artichoke Salad 63

    Oregano Rice 151

    Portobello Soup 44

    Rabbit Cacciatore 107

    Roast Tenderloin of Beef with Madeira Sauce 67

    Shrimp Marsala 119

    Smothered Pork Loin Chops 81

    Spinach Chicken Crêpes 84

    Winter Night Spaghetti with Sausage and Sage 148

N

New England Crab Cakes 113

New Orleans Barbecued Shrimp 117

Nuts

    Apple Cheese Nut Salad 58

    Banana Nut Bread 16

Cashew Salad Dressing 135

Chocolate Chip Zucchini Bread 18

Cold Asparagus with Pecans 129

Glazed Pecan Sprinkles for Salads 54

Graham Cracker Brownies 178

Holiday Sweet Potatoes 160

Nutty Clusters 191

Pecan Cookies 183

Pecan Pie with Kahlúa and Chocolate Chips 163

Powdered Sugar Cookies 182

Praline Pumpkin Pie 163

Quiche with Almonds 12

S&S Tearoom Strawberry Bread 17

Spicy Pecan Cheese Wafers 19

Sugar and Nut Glazed Brie 23

Walnut Cream Sauce 134

White Chocolate Cake with
    Coconut or Praline Topping 168

Wild Rice, Apricot and Almond Salad 57

O

Oatmeal Cake 167

Oatmeal Drop Cookies 180

Old-Fashioned Gingerbread 17

Old-Fashioned Shortbread 179

Oranges and Tangarines

    Citrus Salsa 95

    Fresh Fruit with Poppy Seed Dressing 60

    Kaleidoscope Fruit Salad 192

    Spicy Jicama Salad 62

    Super Salad 61

    Tequila Chicken with Citrus Salsa 95

Oregano Rice 151

P

Paella Salad 150
Party Buffet Marinated Beef Tenderloin 69
Party Salmon Mousse 26
Party Shrimp Mold 31
Pasilla Chicken Enchiladas 93

Pasta

Angel Hair with Red Pepper-Lime Purée 146
Crawfish Tortellini 114
Hunter's Duck Ragu with Pappardelle 105
Italian Chicken 87
Italian Meat Sauce for a Crowd 148
Lasagna Roll-Ups 146
Pasta Nests with Lump Crabmeat 112
Pasta Timbales 147
Penne Mediterraneo Salad 149
Simply Delicious Bow Tie Pasta
    with Garlic and Basil 147
Summer Pasta with Vine Ripe Tomatoes and Basil 149
Vegetable-Beef Stew 51
Winter Night Spaghetti with Sausage and Sage 148

Pavlova 173
Paw Paw's Oysters Rockefeller 120

Peaches

Fruit Jigglers 185
Fruity Shakes 184
Homemade Peach Cobbler 173
Kaleidoscope Fruit Salad 192

Peanut Butter Fingers 193

Pears

French Café Salad 55
Fresh Fruit with Poppy Seed Dressing 60
Fresh Pear and Parmesan Salad 59

Fresh Pear Cake 166
Pecan Cookies 183
Pecan Pie with Kahlúa and Chocolate Chips 163
Peking Spiced Duck 106
Penne Mediterraneo Salad 149
Peppered Duck Breasts 106
Peppered Pork Tenderloin 79
Perini Ranch Steak Rub 139
Pesto and Sun-Dried Tomato Torte 34
Picnic Green Beans 126
Pico de Gallo 143
Pine Nut Crusted Snapper 124

Pineapple

Citrus Salsa 95
Fresh Fruit with Poppy Seed Dressing 60
Hot Pineapple Scallop 23
Kaleidoscope Fruit Salad 192
Tequila Chicken with Citrus Salsa 95

Plum-Mint Sauce 82
Polenta, Tomato and Pesto Casserole 153
Ponzu Marinade 123
Poppy Seed Dressing 60

Pork

Best Baby Back Ribs 80
Eastern North Carolina Pork Barbecue 79
German Style Black-Eyed Peas 127
Glazed Cornish Hens with Savory Stuffing 96
Grilled Honey Glazed Pork Tenderloin 75
Ham and Grits Quiche 13
Honey-Sage Pork Tenderloin 77
Peppered Pork Tenderloin 79
Pork Chops Victoria 81
Pork Tenderloin with Raspberry Sauce 76
Quiche Lorraine 11

Sausage Cheese Biscuits 15

Sherry Marinated Pork Tenderloin 74

Shrimp and Sausage Jambalaya 116

Smothered Pork Loin Chops 81

Spicy Pork Tenderloin with Lime Mayonnaise 78

Sugared Bacon 14

Sweet and Savory Marinated Pork Tenderloin 74

Western Style Baby Back Ribs 80

Winter Night Spaghetti with Sausage and Sage 148

Port, Rosemary and Garlic Marinade 140

Portobello Soup 44

Potatoes

Baked Potato Soup 47

Chunky Creamy Corn Chowder 45

Citrus Baked New Potatoes 157

Corn-Potato Pancakes 156

Gruyère Potato Gratin 157

Jalapeño-Potato Soup 48

Potato Rolls 19

Roasted Lobster-Corn Chowder 46

Sliced Baked Potatoes 158

Vegetable-Beef Stew 51

Whipped Potatoes with a Twist 158

Poultry

Chicken Breasts
with Garlic Balsamic Vinegar Sauce 86

Chicken Dijonnaise 89

Chicken in Roquefort Sauce 89

Chicken Smothered with Onions 85

Chicken with Spicy Peanut Sauce 88

Creamy Poblano Chicken with Cornbread Waffles 92

Cuban Rice and Black Bean Salad 58

Curry Chicken with Tomatoes and Raisins 90

Easy Hawaiian Chicken 90

French Bistro Grilled Chicken 91

Game Day Turkey Tailgate Sandwich 96

Garlic Sour Cream Chicken 87

Glazed Cornish Hens with Savory Stuffing 96

Herb Roasted Chicken Breasts 85

Italian Chicken 87

Mediterranean Chicken 91

Pasilla Chicken Enchiladas 93

Penne Mediterraneo Salad 149

Salsa Chicken Enchiladas 94

Spicy Family Night Meatloaf 73

Spinach Chicken Crêpes 84

Super Easy Crispy Chicken 86

Tequila Chicken with Citrus Salsa 95

Too Easy To Be Tortilla Soup 49

White Chicken Chili 52

Powdered Sugar Cookies 182

Praline Pumpkin Pie 163

Praline Topping 168

Provençal Goat Cheese Gratin 33

Pumpkin

Praline Pumpkin Pie 163

Pumpkin Cake 165

Q

Quiche

Ham and Grits Quiche 13

Quiche Lorraine 11

Quiche with Almonds 12

R

Rabbit Cacciatore 107

Rack of Veal with Garlic and Rosemary 72

Raspberries

Kaleidoscope Fruit Salad 192
Raspberry Glazed Quail 101
Raspberry Sauce 76, 170
White Chocolate Mousse with Raspberry Sauce 170

Red Currant Glaze 108
Rémoulade Sauce 138

Rice

"Best-Ever" Rice 150
Cuban Rice and Black Bean Salad 58
Cumin Rice 151
Fast and Easy Polenta with Roasted Vegetables 154
Glazed Cornish Hens with Savory Stuffing 96
Herbed Couscous with Feta 152
Herbed Wild Rice with Toasted Pine Nuts 152
J.B.'s "Must-Try" Skinny Beans 126
Louisiana Seafood Gumbo 115
Oregano Rice 151
Paella Salad 150
Polenta, Tomato and Pesto Casserole 153
Rice, Black Beans and Feta Salad 57
Shrimp and Sausage Jambalaya 116
Spicy Cajun Shrimp 118
The Best Crawfish Étouffée 113
Wild Rice, Apricot and Almond Salad 57

Roast Quail with Hazelnuts and Port 103
Roast Tenderloin of Beef with Madeira Sauce 67
Roasted Asparagus with Hot Crab Sauce 128
Roasted Lobster-Corn Chowder 46
Rosemary Fried Quail 102

S

S&S Tearoom Strawberry Bread 17

Salad Dressings (see Condiments and Sauces)

Salads

Apple Cheese Nut Salad 58
Cuban Rice and Black Bean Salad 58
French Café Salad 55
Fresh Fruit with Poppy Seed Dressing 60
Fresh Pear and Parmesan Salad 59
Grilled Salmon and Vegetable Salad 122
Kaleidoscope Fruit Salad 192
Marinated Asparagus Salad 63
Marinated Shrimp, Mushroom and Artichoke Salad ... 63
Paella Salad 150
Penne Mediterraneo Salad 149
Rice, Black Beans and Feta Salad 57
Spicy Cole Slaw 53
Spicy Jicama Salad 62
Strawberry Spinach Salad 62
Super Salad 61
Super Simple Slaw 53
Texas Caesar Salad with Cayenne Croutons 56
Warm Cabbage with Saga Blue Cheese 64
Wild Rice, Apricot and Almond Salad 57

Salsa Chicken Enchiladas 94
Salsa Verde 39
Sandwich, Game Day Turkey Tailgate 96
Santa Fe Soufflé 14

Sauces (see Condiments and Sauces)

Sausage Cheese Biscuits 15
Sautéed Salmon with Spinach 121
Savory Northern Italian Quail with Polenta 100
Savory Sage Marinade 110
Savory Sweet Potato Gratin 159

Seafood (also see Fish)

Barbecue Shrimp 116
Crabmeat Cream Puffs 27

Crabmeat Remick 112

Crawfish Tortellini 114

Curried Shrimp Dip 31

Easy and Delicious Crab Mold 32

Fantastic Caviar Torte 30

Favorite Mustard Marinated Shrimp 119

Fresh Corn and Crab Bisque 47

Hot Crab and Artichoke Dip 28

Hot Crab Sauce 128

Jumbo Lump Crabmeat Dip 26

Louisiana Seafood Gumbo 115

Marinated Shrimp, Mushroom
    and Artichoke Salad 63

New England Crab Cakes 113

New Orleans Barbecued Shrimp 117

Paella Salad 150

Party Shrimp Mold 31

Pasta Nests with Lump Crabmeat 112

Paw Paw's Oysters Rockefeller 120

Roasted Asparagus with Hot Crab Sauce 128

Roasted Lobster-Corn Chowder 46

Shellfish Skewers with Asian Dipping Sauce 114

Shrimp and Gruyère Tart 29

Shrimp and Jalapeño Brochettes 118

Shrimp and Sausage Jambalaya 116

Shrimp Ceviche 27

Shrimp Cocktail Acapulco Style 28

Shrimp Marsala 119

Spicy Cajun Shrimp 118

Thanksgiving Oysters 120

The Best Crawfish Étouffée 113

Sherry Marinated Pork Tenderloin 74

Silky Corn Casserole 133

Simply Delicious Bow Tie Pasta
    with Garlic and Basil 147

Sliced Baked Potatoes 158

Smothered Pork Loin Chops 81

Soups

Absolutely Elegant Asparagus Soup 44

Baked Potato Soup 47

Beef Chili 52

Black-Eyed Pea Soup 48

Chunky Creamy Corn Chowder 45

Cream of Roasted Red Pepper Soup 42

Fresh Corn and Crab Bisque 47

Holiday Curried Butternut Soup 45

Jalapeño-Potato Soup 48

Portobello Soup 44

Roasted Lobster-Corn Chowder 46

Southwestern Stew 50

Texas Venison Chili 109

Too Easy To Be Tortilla Soup 49

Tuscan Tomato Soup 43

Vegetable-Beef Stew 51

Very Easy Tuscan White Bean Soup 43

White Chicken Chili 52

Southwestern Poolside Dip 38

Southwestern Stew 50

Spicy Cajun Shrimp 118

Spicy Cole Slaw 53

Spicy Dove Bites 98

Spicy Family Night Meatloaf 73

Spicy Jicama Salad 62

Spicy Peanut Sauce 88

Spicy Pecan Cheese Wafers 19

Spicy Pork Tenderloin with Lime Mayonnaise 78

Spinach

Basil Parmesan Spread 25

Grilled Salmon and Vegetable Salad 122

Lasagna Roll-Ups 146
Last Minute Spinach Balls 25
Pasta Timbales 147
Paw Paw's Oysters Rockefeller 120
Sautéed Salmon with Spinach 121
Spinach Chicken Crêpes 84
Spinach Spoonbread 156
Spinach with Raisins and Pine Nuts 129
Spinach-Artichoke Cheesecake 24
Strawberry Spinach Salad 62
Super Salad 61

Squash
Grilled Salmon and Vegetable Salad 122
Holiday Curried Butternut Soup 45

Strawberries
Fruit Jigglers 185
Fruity Shakes 184
Hot Strawberry Sauce 172
Kaleidoscope Fruit Salad 192
Macaroon Soufflé with Hot Strawberry Sauce 172
S&S Tearoom Strawberry Bread 17
Strawberry Spinach Salad 62

Sugar and Nut Glazed Brie 23
Sugared Bacon 14
Summer Pasta with Vine Ripe Tomatoes and Basil 149
Summertime Tomato Blue Cheese Spread 34
Sun-Dried Tomatoes and Feta Terrine 35
Super Easy Baby Back Ribs 70
Super Easy Beef Brisket 71
Super Easy Crispy Chicken 86
Super Salad 61
Super Simple Slaw 53
Sweet and Savory Marinated Pork Tenderloin 74

Sweet Potatoes
Holiday Sweet Potatoes 160
Savory Sweet Potato Gratin 159

T
Tasty Corn and Green Chili Dip 38
Tequila Chicken with Citrus Salsa 95
Texas Caesar Salad with Cayenne Croutons 56
Texas Venison Chili 109
Thanksgiving Oysters 120
The Best Brussels Sprouts with Bacon 127
The Best Chocolate Pie 162
The Best Crawfish Étouffée 113

Tomatoes
Curry Chicken with Tomatoes and Raisins 90
Dill Cherry Tomatoes 131
Italian Tomato Sauce 29
Pesto and Sun-Dried Tomato Torte 34
Pico de Gallo 143
Polenta, Tomato and Pesto Casserole 153
Salsa Verde 39
Summer Pasta with
Vine Ripe Tomatoes and Basil 149
Summertime Tomato Blue Cheese Spread 34
Sun-Dried Tomatoes and Feta Terrine 35
Tomato Purée 132
Tomato Tart 132
Tomato-Avocado Salsa 142
Tuscan Tomato Soup 43
Vegetable-Beef Stew 51

Too Easy To Be Tortilla Soup 49
Tried and True Pesto 137
Tuscan Tomato Soup 43

V

Veal

    Rack of Veal with Garlic and Rosemary 72

    Veal Cutlets in Mustard Cream Sauce 72

Vegetable-Beef Stew 51

Vegetables (see individual listings)

Venison Backstrap with Savory Sage Marinade 110

Very Easy Tuscan White Bean Soup 43

W

Walnut Cream Sauce 134

Warm Blue Cheese Appetizers 22

Warm Cabbage with Saga Blue Cheese 64

Western Style Baby Back Ribs 80

Whipped Potatoes with a Twist 158

White Chicken Chili 52

White Chocolate Cake
    with Coconut or Praline Topping 168

White Chocolate Mousse with Raspberry Sauce 170

Wild Rice, Apricot and Almond Salad 57

Winter Night Spaghetti with Sausage and Sage............. 148

Wonderful Brownies 178

Z

Zucchini (also see Squash)

    Chocolate Chip Zucchini Bread 18

    Fast and Easy Polenta with Roasted Vegetables 154

    Grilled Salmon and Vegetable Salad 122

    Zucchini au Gratin 131

Women's Auxiliary to Children's Medical Center of Dallas
2777 Stemmons Freeway, Suite 1025 ● Dallas, Texas 75207 ● (214) 456-8371 Cookbook Voice Mail

Please send me _____ copies of
The Collection, Cures for the Common Cuisine @ $25.00/ea _____

Postage & handling   @ $5.00/ea _____

(add $2.50 for each additional book shipped to the same address) _____

TOTAL $ _____

You can also order online at: **www.childrens.com/cookbook**

METHOD OF PAYMENT:
❏ Please make checks payable to:
  Women's Auxiliary to Children's Medical Center
                    OR
❏ Print credit card information below: ❏ Visa   ❏ MasterCard

_____
Name as it appears on card

_____   _____
Card number   Expiration date

_____
Signature

Name _____

Address _____

City/State _____ ZIP _____

Daytime Phone _____

SHIPPING ADDRESS (if different from above):

Address _____

City/State _____ ZIP _____

- -

Women's Auxiliary to Children's Medical Center of Dallas
2777 Stemmons Freeway, Suite 1025 ● Dallas, Texas 75207 ● (214) 456-8371 Cookbook Voice Mail

Please send me _____ copies of
The Collection, Cures for the Common Cuisine @ $25.00/ea _____

Postage & handling   @ $5.00/ea _____

(add $2.50 for each additional book shipped to the same address) _____

TOTAL $ _____

You can also order online at: **www.childrens.com/cookbook**

METHOD OF PAYMENT:
❏ Please make checks payable to:
  Women's Auxiliary to Children's Medical Center
                    OR
❏ Print credit card information below: ❏ Visa   ❏ MasterCard

_____
Name as it appears on card

_____   _____
Card number   Expiration date

_____
Signature

Name _____

Address _____

City/State _____ ZIP _____

Daytime Phone _____

SHIPPING ADDRESS (if different from above):

Address _____

City/State _____ ZIP _____